DANGER
BENEATH THE WAVES

DANGER
BENEATH THE WAVES

A History of the Confederate Submarine
H. L. Hunley

James E. Kloeppel

Sandlapper Publishing, Inc.
Orangeburg, South Carolina

FRONT COVER ILLUSTRATION: The *H. L. Hunley* was the first submarine in history to sink an enemy warship. Manually propelled by its crew of eight men, the *Hunley* sought out and destroyed the USS *Housatonic* on the night of February 17, 1864. This drawing by R. G. Skerrett was based on a painting by Conrad Wise Chapman, which appears in chapter 3.

NOTE: Illustrations appearing in this book, unless otherwise credited, are used courtesy of the United States Naval Historical Center in Washington, D. C.

Library of Congress Cataloging-in-Publication Data
Kloeppel, James E.
    Danger beneath the waves : a history of the Confederate submarine H.L. Hunley / James E. Kloeppel.
        p.   cm.
    Includes bibliographical references and index.
    Summary: Examines the history of the H.L. Hunley, the first submarine to sink an enemy ship, describing its design, construction, operations, and disappearance.
    ISBN 0-87844-096-8   ISBN 0-87844-105-0 (pbk.)
    1. H.L. Hunley (Submarine)—Juvenile literature. 2. United States—History—Civil War, 1861-1865—Naval operations—Submarine—Juvenile literature. 3. Submarine boats—United States—History—19th century—Juvenile literature. [1. H.L. Hunley (Submarine) 2. United States—History—Civil War, 1861-1865—Naval operations—Submarine. 3. Submarines—History—19th century.]
I. Title.
E599.H4K56   1992   91-20426
973.7'57—dc20   CIP
                                                AC

To all submariners who have given their lives
for a cause in which they believed

Preface

More than a century has passed since the fiery hail of lead and iron rained between brothers during the American Civil War. The battle flags have long since been furled, and fallen soldiers, Blue and Gray, have long slept in mute testimony to the hell that swept across this vast country. The four long years of bitter strife as battles raged throughout our divided nation are familiar to all. The actions and reactions of the participants during the many significant events of that terrible struggle have been ably recorded by many historians. While worthy, those events shall not be repeated here. Rather, this book deals with one of the lesser-known events of the Civil War. Lesser known, but far from being less significant, the event was of world-shaking consequence.

During the early years of the Civil War, a group of ingenious Confederates experimented with, and perfected, what newspapers of that time called a "diving torpedo-boat." While extremely primitive, this vessel was by all modern standards a true submarine—the forerunner of today's mighty submarine fleet. With their novel submarine the Confederates successfully attacked and sank the Union warship *Housatonic* on the night of February 17, 1864. For the first time in history a warship was dealt a deathblow by a submarine, an event that would revolutionize marine warfare. The history of this new predator of the seas, the *H. L. Hunley*, will be told on the following pages.

Unfortunately, the facts concerning the *Hunley* are all too often intermingled with fiction, and a certain amount of detective ingenuity is needed to differentiate between the two. Whenever possible, primary sources have been cited and "popular accounts" avoided. Where discrepancies exist between this historical work and other published accounts, they are duly noted. In some instances where no reliable historical documentation could be found, future research might disprove portions of this text.

The author wishes to gratefully acknowledge the guidance and support graciously offered to him by the following individuals and institutions: Richard H. F. Lindemann, Reference Archivist, and the staff of the Robert W. Woodruff Library of Emory University; Wilbur E. Meneray, Head of Rare Books and Manuscripts at the Howard-Tilton Memorial Library of Tulane University; Rose Lambert of the Louisiana Historical Center; Timothy J. Chester, Chief Curator of the Louisiana State Museum; Robert Zollars, Director of the Submarine Force Library and Museum; Marlene Judy of the Engineering Library of the U.S. Army Corps of Engineers at Charleston; Norlin Library of the University of Colorado; Library of Congress; National Archives; Naval History Library; Georgia Institute of Technology; and the South Carolina Historical Society. Thanks also go to Rick Holcombe, Robbin Plesher, and Paula Burch for their aid and support. A special note of thanks to my wonderful wife, Darlene, for her love, understanding, and support.

Contents

1

Beginnings and the CSS *Pioneer*

At New Orleans, in 1862, we built the first boat. She was made of iron 1/4-inch thick. The boat was of a cigar shape, 30 feet long and 4 feet in diameter. This boat demonstrated to us the fact that we could construct a boat that would move at will in any direction desired, and at any distance from the surface.

—James McClintock

At the outbreak of the American Civil War, the South found itself facing an adversary of far superior military strength. The North possessed an established army and navy, both well equipped with the accoutrements of war. The South, barely able to equip an army, lacked even a single vessel with which it could form a navy. When hostilities turned to war, the Confederacy was forced to rely upon private assistance until ships could be built or purchased and a navy thereby formed. Thus, immediately following President Lincoln's call for seventy-five thousand volunteers to quell the "insurrection in the South," Southern President Jefferson Davis issued a proclamation inviting applications for a letter of marque and reprisal, a privateer's license granted by the Confederate government.

Privateering, a practice almost as old as the sea itself, was believed distinct from piracy and had been used for centuries by many countries during times of war. To raise an emergency cruising force, governments would grant commissions to privately owned vessels, authorizing them to capture or destroy enemy vessels and cargo. Captured ships and cargo became the property of the owners and crew of the privateer, and could be sold at handsome profits.

To prevent privateering from degenerating into piracy, as had happened so often in the past, privateers were strictly monitored by the Confederate government. Applicants were required to accurately describe their vessel, its armament, and the number of officers and crew members. The names of the vessel's owners had to be listed and an appropriate bond posted.[1]

Defenseless merchantmen, easy to capture and to dispose of, were the natural prey of privateers. The Confederate government, however, severely lacking naval military strength, needed the further aid of privateers in attacking the warships of the Federal fleet. As an incentive for the greater risks involved, the Confederate government offered a lucrative bounty equal to 20 percent of the total value of each warship destroyed.

The South realized that privateering was not the total solution to the naval dilemma; it was merely a temporary measure intended to ward off the Federal fleet until an adequate navy could be formed. But, with the limited resources available in the South, it was questionable whether an adequate navy could be formed within a reasonable length of time.

Northern economic and industrial strength, so essential to mobilizing a successful war effort, far surpassed that of the South. Primarily agricultural in nature, the South lacked the heavy industry and trades so readily found in the North. Numerous factories capable of wartime production of military goods were located in the North but were virtually nonexistent in the South. Furthermore, in terms of manpower the North again had a great advantage. Nearly twenty-three million people lived in the North, compared to only nine million—of whom approximately three million were slaves—in the South.

Only by developing modern war machinery could the South place its naval military power on a parity with the North's. Severely lacking in many respects, the South was therefore open to new thoughts and inventions that had been largely ignored by the North. Among these were an ambitious ironclad program, implementation of torpedoes both offensively and defensively, and the construction of torpedo boats and submarines. Hoping these new developments in naval warfare would offset the great disparity in numbers and naval strength, the South went to war.

The concept of submarine warfare, successfully developed and proven during the Civil War, was not new. Indeed, people had entertained thoughts of building a vessel to travel beneath the waves for centuries. In 1578 an Englishman named William Bourne published the first written account detailing the design of such a machine. His *Inventions and Devices* describes a clever contraption to be constructed of wood and leather, capable of being submerged and propelled underwater. According to Bourne, the vessel's displacement (and hence its buoyancy) could be controlled by simply expanding or contracting the flexible sides of the hull. Ingenious as the design was, the vessel apparently was never built.

Forty-two years later, Cornelius van Drebbel, a Dutch physician living in England, developed the first working submarine. During the years 1620 through 1624, Drebbel built three diving boats, which he successfully demonstrated in the River Thames. But due to lack of public or military interest, Drebbel's submarines remained a mere curiosity.

In 1776, during the American Revolution, a young Yale student named David Bushnell built a simple, but very functional, one-man submarine. The wooden hull of the novel craft was shaped like two giant tortoise shells stuck together. Appropriately named the *Turtle*, the vessel measured over 7 feet long, 8 feet deep, and 4 feet wide.

The *Turtle* was maneuvered by two hand-cranked propellers, one for horizontal movement and the other for vertical. The vessel's depth could be controlled by means of a ballast tank and two hand-operated force pumps. A brass snorkel assembly drew in fresh air while the vessel was operating just below the water's surface.

In early September of 1776, under cover of darkness, Sergeant Ezra Lee (whom Bushnell had personally trained) secretly maneuvered the

Turtle under the HMS *Eagle*, the sixty-four-gun flagship of the British fleet. But attempts to screw a magazine of gunpowder into the huge warship's hull failed, and Lee was forced to abandon the plan.

Twenty years after Sergeant Lee's brave attempt with the *Turtle*, American inventor Robert Fulton (then residing in France) produced a similarly remarkable submarine, the 21-foot *Nautilus*. Fulton's innovative design included a hollow keel ballast tank, diving fins, and a hand-driven propeller for submerged operations, and a collapsible mast and sail for operating upon the water's surface.

Fulton tried to sell his design first to France, then to England, and finally Russia. When his efforts failed, Fulton returned to the United States and diverted his creative genius to the production of practical steam-powered boats. Interestingly, in 1815 the inventor was once again dabbling with submarine construction. Unfortunately, Fulton died before his new vessel was completed, and the 80-foot behemoth was scrapped.

In 1848, when tensions between Germany and Denmark erupted into war, a young German named Wilhelm Bauer stepped forward with a bold plan to disrupt the Danish fleet using a submarine. With support from the German military, Bauer's *Sea Diver* quickly took shape. Hammered out of sheet iron, the vessel was 25 feet long, 6 feet wide, and 9 feet deep. It was powered by two men spinning treadmills connected to a screw propeller.

The mere presence of this strange and intimidating diving machine, lumbering mischievously along the surface of the water, was sufficient to repulse the entire Danish fleet, albeit temporarily.

Several years later, during the Crimean War, Bauer received funds from Russia to build another, larger submarine. Launched in 1855, the *Sea Devil* measured 52 feet long, 12 feet wide, and 11 feet deep. Like its predecessor, the vessel relied on muscle-power (its crew numbered thirteen) and resembled a slightly flattened sausage of sheet iron. Although the *Sea Devil* never saw military action, Bauer reportedly made over one hundred dives in the vessel, at depths ranging up to 150 feet.

For nearly three hundred years, the full destructive potential of the

This daguerreotype of James R. McClintock, designer of three Civil War submarines, was taken in the 1850s or early 1860s. McClintock is said to have run away from home at the age of eleven to become a cabin boy on a river packet. Pulling himself up by the bootstraps, McClintock later became a steamboat captain. Self-educated in mechanical subjects, McClintock operated a machine shop with Baxter Watson in New Orleans when the Civil War began.

submarine had never been truly demonstrated, only imagined. But the time was rapidly approaching when the submarine would indeed prove itself in battle.

Two men instrumental in the South's development of a functioning submarine were James R. McClintock and Baxter Watson. These men, both experienced machinists and marine engineers, operated a shop in New Orleans, Louisiana, where they manufactured steam-gauges and other pieces of machinery. Their combined talents and creative genius were well known to local residents. The *New Orleans Daily Delta* for August 17, 1861, stated:

> Watson and McClintock, steam-gauge makers, at 31 Front Levee, have turned their inventive genius to good account.
>
> They have ingeniously overcome the great difficulties heretofore encountered in the making of cold-pressed Minie and other leaden balls.
>
> They have built their own machine, and have brought it to such perfection that they can now turn out 10,000 Minie-balls of perfect and uniform shape per hour.
>
> Such are some of the results, almost directly, of the blockade. They relate particularly to the necessities of the time.
>
> There are many others, notice of which we shall defer to another time.
>
> We might also say that the ingenuity and enterprise of our citizens have been developed to a degree which will enable us to raise the blockade of our port at will.

While it is not clear which of the two men conceived the idea, sometime in 1861 Watson and McClintock began constructing an underwater boat, or submarine. The last paragraph of the preceding *Daily Delta* article may have been referring to the development of such a vessel. Intending to outfit their novel boat as a privateer, Watson and McClintock planned to attack vessels of the Federal blockading fleet that were then gathering downriver from New Orleans. The partners hoped the submarine, hidden from view while gliding beneath the waves, would silently approach victims and destroy them with torpedoes—explosives that could be pushed or pulled into the side of an enemy vessel and detonated.

The unique design and purpose of the vessel placed stringent demands upon its builders. The new boat was to be built entirely from iron yet had to be completely watertight. The queer little craft had to be stable both on and below the water's surface. Additionally, for underwater operations a steam engine was totally out of the question, and the primitive electric motors available at that time lacked sufficient power to propel the submarine. Therefore, the vessel had to be strong enough to withstand the pressure of operating below the surface, yet light enough so it could be propelled manually by the small crew.

Little is known concerning the actual construction of the submarine. According to local legend, Watson and McClintock built their boat at the well-known Leeds Foundry on the corner of Fourcher and DeLord streets. The vessel was completed in the early part of 1862; appropriately christened the *Pioneer*, it was launched at the Government Yard on the New Basin in February.[2]

Under the command of a man named John K. Scott, the *Pioneer* began trial operations in Lake Pontchartrain. During one test it destroyed a barge placed as a target, blowing fragments "so high that only a few splinters were heard from."[3] Indeed, the *Pioneer* seemed to possess only one minor problem. Lacking a periscope, the vessel was steered by a compass "which acted so slow that the boat would at times alter her course for one or two minutes before it would be discovered, thus losing the direct course, and so compel the operator to come to the top of the water more frequently that he otherwise would."[4] Convinced of the seaworthiness of the novel vessel, Commander Scott applied for a letter of marque to make the *Pioneer* the first submarine privateer in history:

> Application is hereby made for a commission or authority in the name of the Government of these States, to issue to the undersigned as commander of the submarine boat called the *Pioneer* for authority to cruise the high seas, bays, rivers, estuaries, etc., in the name of the Government, and aid said Government by the destruction or capture of any and all vessels opposed to or at war with said Confederate States, and

to aid in repelling its enemies.

Said vessel is commanded by John K. Scott, who is a citizen of New Orleans and of this confederacy. Said vessel was built at New Orleans in the year 1862; is a propeller; is 34 feet in length; is 4 feet breadth; is 4 feet deep. She measures about 4 tons; has round conical ends and is painted black. She is owned by Robert R. Barrow, Baxter Watson, and James R. McClintock, all of this city of New Orleans. She will carry a magazine of explosive matter, and will be manned by two men or more.

And I hereby promise to be vigilant and zealous in employing said vessel for the purpose aforesaid and abide by all laws and instructions and at all times acknowledge the authority of the Government of said States and its lawful agent and officers.[5]

According to the register of commissions issued to applicants for letters of marque and reprisal kept at the Custom-House Collector's Office in New Orleans, John Scott was indeed granted a commission for the *Pioneer* on March 31, 1862. The *Pioneer* was officially described as a "submarine propeller" and its armament as a "magazine of explosives." The commission was granted upon a $5,000 bond, the sureties being Horace L. Hunley and Henry J. Leovy.

Unfortunately, it is no longer known why or even when Hunley and Leovy became involved with the *Pioneer.* It is also not clear to what extent multimillionaire Robert R. (Ruffin) Barrow, listed as one of the owners in the preceding document, was actually involved. Barrow was Hunley's brother-in-law, having married Volumnia Washington Hunley on February 7, 1850.[6] But beyond their experiences with the *Pioneer,* apparently neither Leovy nor Barrow were to have any further involvement with submarine vessels.

Horace Lawson Hunley, however, would become a leading figure in submarine development: a development culminating in the first successful submarine attack upon an enemy warship. Hunley was born in Sumner County, Tennessee, on December 29, 1823, but eight years later his family moved to New Orleans.[7] He received a bachelor of law degree from Tulane University in 1849, and later became assistant deputy collector at the Custom-House. Perhaps it was while serving in this capacity that Hunley became involved with the *Pioneer.*

After receiving a commission for the *Pioneer,* Commander Scott and the owners were no doubt eager to place the submarine in operation against the enemy fleet gathered outside New Orleans. A lucrative bounty could be anticipated for each blockader the tiny *Pioneer* could sink. But the *Pioneer* was not to return one cent of its owners' investment, for the *Pioneer* was never to prove itself in battle.

Some writers have claimed that the *Pioneer's* operations came to an abrupt end when it became unmanageable in some way and sank, along with the crew. However, this appears not to have been the case. In a letter written after the war, James R. McClintock claimed: "The evacuation of New Orleans lost this boat before our experiments were completed . . ." William Alexander, later intimately associated with the *Pioneer's* successor, the *Hunley,* sheds more light on the subject: "Shortly before the capture of New Orleans by the United States troops, Captain Hunley, James McClintock, and Baxter Watson were engaged in building a submarine torpedo-boat in the New Basin of that city. The city falling into the hands of the Federals before it was completed, the boat was sunk, and these gentlemen came to Mobile."[8]

Captain David G. Farragut, flag-officer of the Union's West Gulf Blockading Squadron, pushed his ships past Forts Jackson and St. Philip on the lower Mississippi and captured New Orleans in April 1862. So it appears that scarcely one month after being granted a letter of marque, the *Pioneer,* the first submarine privateer, was scuttled to prevent it from falling into enemy hands.

In 1878, outside New Orleans, while digging a canal along the Lake Pontchartrain shoreline just west of Spanish Fort, a relic was discovered by workers on the dredgeboat *Valentine.* The object, which resembled an old steam boiler, was unceremoniously deposited on the shore and quickly forgotten.

Seventeen years later, on a summer's day in 1895, Alfred Wellborn and three other boys were strolling along the marshy shores of Lake Pontchartrain. They stumbled upon an iron object hidden by tangled underbrush and partially sunk in the mud. The object looked like a boat, and young Alfred suspected it was one of the submarines constructed by the Confederacy during the war. The boys told a group of men who were building a wharf nearby of their exciting discovery, but the men seemed only mildly interested. Returning several months later, however, Alfred was surprised to find that the boat had been recovered and placed on exhibit at nearby Spanish Fort.[9]

Interest in the relic proved to be short-lived, however. When Alfred Wellborn again visited Spanish Fort on a fishing excursion in 1907, he found the forgotten boat lying on its side surrounded by tall weeds. Dismayed over the vessel's decay, Wellborn was moved to write the *New Orleans Times-Democrat* on June 19, 1907:

> Several years ago there was lying among the ruins of Spanish Fort an old cigar-shaped iron boat, which was quite rusty, but still in a fair state of preservation, considering that it had been left for years exposed to the weather and to anyone who might care to take parts of it. I was told that this was one of the old submarine boats built during the War Between the States.
>
> It seems surprising, if this is a fact, that this old submarine should be left on the canal bank to decay, when all relics of the Confederacy are eagerly sought for, and as we have a hall in our city to shelter all these old relics.
>
> In this day when the whole world is interested in building up its navies, it should be of pride for all Southern people to collect all that belonged to the Confederate Navy, which did so much to revolutionize the naval architecture of the world. . . .
>
> I understand that this old boat is still at Spanish Fort, on the banks of the canal, and that it is fast going to ruin. It would be an easy matter to place the old relic on a barge or schooner and bring it to the city, where it would be a valuable acquisition to the Howard Memorial Museum.[10]

Public interest finally awakened and people demanded an appropriate resting place for the relic. The *New Orleans Picayune* for April 2, 1909, states: "It was decided last night at a special meeting of Camp Beauregard . . . to hold special exercises at the presentation to the Soldiers' Home of the old Confederate submarine torpedo-boat which

Courtesy of the Naval Historical Foundation

Long purported to be the Pioneer, *the predecessor of the* Hunley, *this relic was recovered at New Orleans in 1878 by workers on the dredgeboat* Valentine. *While modern research proves it is not the* Pioneer, *the vessel's true identity, and that of its builders, remains a mystery. William Morrison Robinson, Jr., took this photograph in 1926 while the relic was exhibited at Camp Nicholls, the Confederate Soldiers' Home on the banks of Bayou St. John.*

was last week removed from Spanish Fort to Camp Nicholls. . . . When the New Orleans Terminal Company bought the property at the fort, it donated the boat to Camp Beauregard, and the Camp, in turn, through Commandant W. O. Hart, presented it to the Soldiers' Home. Last week it was removed to the Home, and will be officially presented on April 10."

Camp Nicholls, located on the banks of Bayou St. John, was the Louisiana State Home for Confederate Soldiers. There the submarine's keel was embedded in a concrete base and she remained on display for many years. Writer and historian William Morrison Robinson, Jr., critically examined the relic in February 1926. In his book *The Confederate Privateers*, Robinson provided an excellent description of the vessel:

> She is an even 20 feet in length over all, her greatest inside width is but 3 feet 2 inches, and her maximum depth is 6 feet. In plan view her curves are very pleasing. In midship cross-section, she suggests a racing yacht model. She is fabricated of 1/4-inch iron sheets, fastened with 5/8-inch countersunk rivets. The deck plates are curved to conic sections.
>
> The propeller—the blades are now broken off—was turned by cranks operated by two men, sitting on little iron brackets fastened, opposite, on each side of the vessel, immediately under the hatchway. There were rudders on either end, connected for single control. The bow rudder is gone, the stock being snapped off just below the rudder-post. The stern rudder is buried in the concrete base, but a photograph taken before the emplacement shows it to be an equipoise-rudder. The diving was accomplished by two side vanes, or fins, 35 inches long by 16 inches wide, placed about on the level of the propeller and over the forward rudder. They both worked on the same shaft, rotated by a lever arm, which directly pointed the angle of the dive. The port vane has been twisted off.
>
> The sole entrance to the vessel is through the 18-inch hatchway amidships. The edge of the opening is reinforced with an iron collar, 3/8-inch thick and 2 1/2 inches wide. The cover is gone, but the indications are that it was simply a lid hinged aft and closing on a gasket fastened directly to the curved roof or deck; for the rivet holes surrounding the hatch are only 1/8-inch in diameter. It does not seem probable that the cover stood high enough, as in the *Hunley*, to serve as a conning tower with eyeports. In

fact, little provision seems to have been made for light or observation. In the roof, forward of the hatch, there are two groups of eight 3/4-inch holes, each, arranged in circles one foot in diameter. These holes may have been glassed, serving as small light-ports. Surmounting the center of the more forward set of holes is a cuff, five inches in height and in diameter, which seems to have been a stuffing box through which an air shaft passed. . . . There is in the prow or nose of the vessel a 2-inch circular opening, which, I am inclined to believe, was used for forward observation rather than as a socket for a torpedo spar.[11]

On April 24, 1957, the submarine was sent on its final journey. Acquired by the Louisiana State Museum, the vessel was moved to the arcade of the Presbytere, just outside Jackson Square in New Orleans. Now protected by the museum, it is finally safe from the elements.

For many years this relic has been purported to be the *Pioneer*, predecessor of the *Hunley*. New evidence, however, indicates the *Pioneer* was actually sold at auction in 1868, ten years before an entirely different vessel was discovered along the Lake Pontchartrain shoreline. How did this case of mistaken identity occur?

When William Alexander's moving account of his adventures with the *Hunley* appeared in the June 29, 1902, edition of the *New Orleans Picayune*, the relic lay rusting on its side at Spanish Fort. Surprisingly, it was Alexander's story—or rather the stories that followed it—that first led to misidentifying the relic as the *Pioneer*.

"Visitors to Spanish Fort may still see, half submerged in the weeds and flowers growing on the banks of Bayou St. John, a rusty vessel of curious shape," read the *Picayune*. "It was, as stated in the accompanying narrative, built during the war by Captain Hunley as a submarine torpedo-boat, and though never used in battle, is the prototype of the vessel which subsequently destroyed the Federal cruiser *Housatonic*."

This is simply incorrect. Alexander's narrative did not state, as the *Picayune* writer claimed, that the vessel at Spanish Fort was the boat Hunley built. Indeed, Alexander never mentioned the relic at all. It was the newspaper writer's recklessness that magically transformed the relic

Another view of the submarine mistakenly identified as the Pioneer, *photographed by William Morrison Robinson, Jr., in 1926. The relic remained on display, unprotected, for many years at the Confederate Soldiers' Home. Today the old submarine is part of the Louisiana State Museum, resting near Jackson Square in the arcade of the Presbytere.*

into the *Pioneer.* And to some extent, one can understand why the public believed him. The relic was found close to the right place at close to the right time. One submarine was lost and one submarine had been found. That the vessel should be the *Pioneer* was not outrageous.

In his postwar letter to Matthew Fontaine Maury, James McClintock claimed the *Pioneer* "was of a cigar shape, 30 feet long and 4 feet in diameter." These values are in close agreement with those given by John Scott in his application for a letter of marque. There the vessel is described as being "34 feet long, 4 feet deep, 4 feet wide, with round conical ends."

The Confederate government was strict about applications concerning privateers. The vessel's dimensions duly stated by the applicant had to be exact, not guessed at or approximated. While McClintock's memory might be called into question, there is no reason to doubt the values given by Scott.

The relic, however, on display in New Orleans was measured by William Robinson and found to be 20 feet long, 6 feet deep, and 3 feet wide. These values are significantly different from the dimensions given by both McClintock and Scott.

The descriptions do not match either. "In plan view her curves are

Courtesy of the Naval Historical Foundation

very pleasing," wrote Robinson. "In midship cross-section, she suggests a racing yacht model." This is a far cry from the "cigar-shaped" vessel described by McClintock, or the submarine with round conical ends listed in Scott's application.

Surprisingly, a vessel fully matching the description and dimensions of the *Pioneer* was recovered by the Federals during the occupation of New Orleans. This intriguing piece of evidence comes from an article entitled "Submarine Torpedo Boats" written by Rear Admiral G. W. Baird in the 1902 *Journal of American Societies of Naval Engineers*.

When a Third Assistant on board the *Pensacola* during the Civil War, I had the pleasure of assisting Second Assistant Engineer Alfred Colin in the measurements and drawings of a submarine torpedo boat which had been fished out of the canal near the "New Basin," between New Orleans and the Lake Pontchartrain. Mr. Colin's drawing was sent by the Fleet Engineer (Mr. Shock) to the Navy Department.

The boat was built of iron cut from old boilers. . . . She was 30 feet in length; the middle body was cylindrical, 10 feet long, and the ends were conical. She had a little conning tower with a manhole in the top and small, circular, glass windows in its sides. She was propelled by a screw, which was operated by one man. . . .

Mr. McClintock (whom I met after the Civil War had ended) informed me that he made several descents in his boat, in the lake, and succeeded in destroying a small schooner and several rafts. He stated that the U.S. Steamers *New London* and *Calhoun* had been a menace on the lake, and this gave rise to the torpedo boat; but before an attack was made the fleet of Farragut had captured New Orleans, and his boat was sunk to prevent her falling into the hands of the enemy. His boat required but two men to operate it. . . . He frankly stated that the model of the boat was improper, in that the small displacement afforded by the sharp ends was insufficient to keep the boat on even keel if a man moved a few inches forward or aft, and that this was a serious objection.[12]

What became of this remarkable submarine, pulled from a canal during the Civil War and critically examined by the Federals? The morning edition of the *New Orleans Picayune* for February 15, 1868, provides part of the answer: "A torpedo boat, which was built in this city or hereabouts during the war, and which is now lying on the banks of the New Canal, near Claiborne Street, is to be sold at public auction today, by the United States authorities, at 12 o'clock, at the Canal street entrance of the Custom House. The boat in question, which is built of iron and weighs about two tons, was sunk in the Canal about the time of the occupation of the city by the Federal forces, in 1862. It was built as an experiment, and was never fully perfected, and is only valuable now for the machinery and iron which is in and about it." The *Picayune* afternoon edition claimed the submarine was indeed sold . . . for $43.

As yet, no record has been found indicating what happened to this priceless relic after the sale. Perhaps this submarine, the real *Pioneer*, was reduced to scrap iron by the blows of a junk dealer's hammer. Possibly some day more will be known.

Ten years after the *Pioneer* was auctioned off, an entirely different vessel—the one now on display in the Presbytere—was pulled from the water by the *Valentine's* workers. But where was this mysterious submarine built? Who financed its construction?

Perhaps the submarine was a war trophy hauled to New Orleans by the Federals during the city's occupation. Or maybe it was taken there at an early date by the Confederates in hopes of attacking the blockading fleet. Indeed, the relic bears a striking resemblance to an illustration that appeared in *Harper's Weekly* on November 2, 1861, which shows a Confederate submarine allegedly prowling the waters off Norfolk, Virginia.

Unfortunately, whatever definite knowledge once existed about this mysterious vessel or its builders has thus far been lost to history. However, a passage that might relate to this vessel appears in a book written by Simon Lake.[13] In writing about the relic at Camp Nicholls, Lake claimed:

> The New Orleans submarine boat was also built by the Confederates during the Civil War. A friend who took the photograph of this vessel told

me the following story as related to him by a Southern gentleman who was familiar with the history of the boat. It appears that this submarine was the conception of a wealthy planter who owned a number of slaves. He thought that it would add considerable interest to the occasion of her launching if, when the vessel left the ways, she should disappear beneath the waves and make a short run beneath the surface before coming up. So he took two of his most intelligent slaves and instructed them how to hold the tiller when the vessel slid down the ways, and in which way to turn the propeller for a time after she began to lose her launched speed. He told them when they got ready to come up they should push the tiller down and the vessel would come to the surface to be towed ashore.

A great crowd assembled to see this novel launching. "When things were all ready," said the old Southern gentleman, "sure enough, them two [slaves] got into the boat and shut down the hatches; and do you know, suh, that at that time them [slaves] was worth a thousand dollars apiece." Well, it seems that the boat slid down the ways and disappeared under the water just as had been planned. The crowd waited expectantly, but the vessel did not reappear. Eventually they got into boats and put out hooks and grappling lines, but she could not be found. The designer of the craft stated as his opinion that "he might have known better than to trust them pesky [slaves] anyway," and he was willing to bet that they had taken the opportunity to steal the vessel and run away. He asserted that very likely they would take the boat up North and give it to the Yankees, and that they could expect to hear of the Yanks' using it to blow up some of their own (Confederate) ships.

Her disappearance remained a mystery for a great many years—until long after the war closed, in fact, and the incident had been forgotten. Years afterward, during some dredging operations to deepen the harbor, the dredge buckets one day got hold of something they could not lift. A diver was sent down to investigate, and he reported that there was some metal object buried in the mud which looked like a steam boiler. They set to work to raise this, and putting chains around it they lifted it on to the wharf. The old gentleman, in closing the narrative, remarked, "And do you know, suh, when they opened the hatch them two blamed [slaves] was still in thar, but they warn't wuth a [darned] cent."

Long rejected by historians as being a canard, the preceding account may, in fact, contain elements of truth after all. While some writers claimed the *Pioneer* sank in New Orleans, killing her crew, the accounts of James McClintock, William Alexander, and Admiral Baird negate this claim. Perhaps historians, in writing about such a sinking with loss of life, were unknowingly referring to this second, unidentified vessel. According to Lake's account, this second vessel did sink, claiming the lives of at least two men.

Additional support for these theories is found in a later passage of Simon Lake's book. Once again referring to the relic on display in New Orleans, Lake, a noted authority on submarines at the turn of the century, claimed the vessel would not float. "It is evident that the designer of this vessel miscalculated and made his boat so much overweight that she could not be given sufficient buoyancy to bring her to the surface by the means provided," he wrote. "From a study of the form of this vessel, she should have been very stable, and I am of the opinion that she could have been successfully navigated submerged had she been properly ballasted."[14]

This is the final proof needed to bring a discussion of the *Pioneer* to an end. If, as Simon Lake contends, the vessel on display in New Orleans lacked sufficient buoyancy to float on the water's surface, one fact becomes unmistakably clear: said vessel is definitely not the *Pioneer*. The *Pioneer* not only floated, but successfully dived and surfaced numerous times in Lake Pontchartrain. According to McClintock: "This boat demonstrated to us the fact that we could construct a boat that would move at will in any direction desired, and at any distance from the surface." Additionally, if Lake is correct that the vessel on display would not float, this adds credibility to his earlier story regarding the vessel's launching. Being grossly overweight, when launched it immediately sank below the waves, taking its crew to a watery grave. Perhaps one day more will be known of the relic's history.

As for the *Pioneer*, unable to reverse Captain Farragut's capture of New Orleans, it was unceremoniously sunk by the builders to prevent its secret from falling into Federal hands. Disappointed, the builders fled to Mobile.

2

Operations of the CSS *Hunley*

Charleston and its defenders will occupy the most conspicuous place in the history of the war, and it shall be as much
glory as I shall wish if I can inscribe myself as one of its
defenders.

—Lieutenant George E. Dixon

In 1862 the city of Mobile, Alabama, was under the command of an
imaginative officer, Major General Dabney H. Maury. Having a keen
interest in projects involving underwater torpedoes, Maury fully supported Hunley and McClintock's plan to build another submarine. He
granted permission to construct the vessel at the machine shop of
Thomas W. Parks and Thomas B. Lyons. Additionally, Maury offered
technical assistance in the form of Lieutenant George E. Dixon and
William A. Alexander. These two young engineers from the Twenty-
first Alabama Infantry were detached from special duty at the shop
to assist with the design and construction of the submarine.

This venture was apparently named the *American Diver,* and Horace
L. Hunley—now a firm supporter of submarines—bore the entire cost
of its construction alone. The new vessel was built of boiler iron and
was similar in shape to the *Pioneer.* According to Alexander, the "cross
section was oblong, about 25 feet long, tapering at each end, 5 feet
wide, and 6 feet deep."[1] McClintock, however, claimed that "to obtain
room for machinery and persons, she was built 36 feet long, 3 feet

21

Horace Lawson Hunley, shown in this undated photograph, was a New Orleans cotton merchant, lawyer, legislator, and submarine promoter. Hunley's interest in submarines began with the Pioneer *and continued through the building and launching of two subsequent craft.*

wide, and 4 feet high. Twelve feet of each end was built tapering . . . to make her easy to pass through the water."[2]

Whatever its dimensions, the *American Diver* had serious problems. "There was much time and money lost in efforts to build an electromagnetic engine for propelling this boat, but without success," wrote McClintock. "I afterwards fitted cranks to turn the propeller by hand, working four men at a time. But, the air being so close and the work so hard, we were unable to get a speed sufficient to make the boat of service against vessels blockading this port.[3]

Originally designed for electric propulsion, the submarine proved awkward to handle and extremely difficult to propel manually. Nevertheless, an attempt was made with the *American Diver* to attack the Federal fleet gathered outside Mobile Bay, resulting in near disaster. "It was towed off Fort Morgan, intending to man it there and attack the blockading fleet outside," wrote Alexander, "but the weather was rough, and with a heavy sea the boat became unmanageable and finally sunk, but no lives were lost."[4] The *American Diver* had dived its last. Sunk somewhere off Fort Morgan in Mobile Bay, it remains there to this day.

Disappointed, but not discouraged, Hunley decided to build yet a third submarine. To raise the necessary capital, Hunley chose to sell shares in the submarine torpedo boat. Retaining one-third ownership for himself, Hunley sold the remaining $10,000 interest in the vessel to four members of a special engineer corps engaged in "the special service of destroying the enemy's property by torpedoes and similar inventions."[5] E. C. Singer purchased a $5,000 share, R. W. Dunn bought a $2,000 share, and B. A. Whitney and J. D. Breaman together bought a $3,000 share.[6]

Given the fact that Hunley could easily have financed the project alone, his decision to sell shares seems odd, and it is even more perplexing when we consider another fact regarding the investors. As members of the special engineer corps, the men were to receive 50 percent of the value of all property destroyed by their inventions. Thus it appears a profit motive may have influenced the building and financing of the submarine.

The new submarine was constructed in the spring of 1863 in the Parks and Lyons machine shop. The builders "took more pains with her model and machinery," wrote McClintock, designing the vessel expressly for hand power. Its crew would consist of nine individuals; eight men to turn the crank connected to the propeller, and one man to steer and direct its operations.[7] It was christened the *H. L. Hunley* in honor of its supporter Horace Lawson Hunley. Fortunately, William Alexander left a detailed description of this fascinating vessel:

> We decided to build another boat, and for this purpose took a cylinder boiler which we had on hand, 48 inches in diameter and 25 feet long (all dimensions are from memory). We cut this boiler in two, longitudinally, and inserted two 12-inch boiler-iron strips in her sides; lengthened her by one tapering course fore and aft, to which were attached bow and stern castings, making the boat about 30 feet long, 4 feet wide, and 5 feet deep. A longitudinal strip 12 inches wide was riveted the full length on top. At each end a bulkhead was riveted across to form water-ballast tanks (unfortunately these were left open on top); they were used in raising and sinking the boat. In addition to these water tanks the boat was ballasted by flat castings, made to fit the outside bottom of the shell and fastened thereto by 'Tee' headed bolts passing through stuffing boxes inside the boat, the inside end of the bolt squared to fit a wrench, that the bolts might be turned and the ballast dropped, should the necessity arise.
>
> In connection with each of the water tanks there was a sea-cock open to the sea to supply the tank for sinking; also a force pump to eject the water from the tanks in the sea for raising the boat to the surface. There was also a bilge connection to the pump. A mercury gauge, open to the sea, was attached to the shell near the forward tank, to indicate the depth of the boat below the surface. A 1 1/4-inch shaft passed through stuffing boxes on each side of the boat, just forward of the end of the propeller shaft. On each end of this shaft, outside of the boat, castings, or lateral fins, 5 feet long and 8 inches wide, were secured. This shaft was operated by a lever amidships, and by raising or lowering the ends of these fins, operated as the fins of a fish, changing the depth of the boat below the surface at will, without disturbing the water level in the ballast tanks.

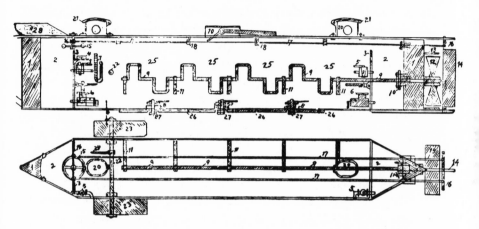

Diagram of the inner workings of the Hunley, *based on a sketch by William A. Alexander.*

KEY:

1) BOW AND STERN CASTINGS
2) WATER BALLAST TANKS
3) TANK BULKHEADS
4) COMPASS
5) SEA-COCKS
6) PUMPS
7) MERCURY GAUGE
8) KEEL BALLAST STUFFING BOXES
9) PROPELLER SHAFT AND CRANKS
10) STERN BEARING AND GLAND
11) SHAFT BRACES
12) PROPELLER
13) WROUGHT RING AROUND PROPELLER
14) RUDDER
15) STEERING WHEEL
16) STEERING LEVER
17) STEERING RODS
18) ROD BRACES
19) AIR BOX
20) HATCHWAYS
21) HATCH COVERS
22) SHAFT OF SIDE FINS
23) SIDE FINS
24) SHAFT LEVER
25) CREW STATION
26) CAST IRON KEEL BALLAST
27) BOLTS
28) TORPEDO BOOM

The rudder was operated by a wheel, and levers connected to rods passing through stuffing boxes in the stern castings, and operated by the captain or pilot forward. An adjusted compass was placed in front of the forward tank. The boat was operated by manual power, with an ordinary propeller. On the propeller shaft there were formed eight cranks at different angles; the shaft was supported by brackets on the starboard side, the men sitting on the port side turning on the cranks. The propeller shaft and cranks took up so much room that it was very difficult to pass fore and aft, and when the men were in their places this was next to impossible. In operation, one half of the crew had to pass through the fore hatch, the other through the after hatchway. The propeller revolved in a wrought iron ring or band, to guard against a line being thrown in to foul it.

There were two hatchways—one fore and one aft—16 inches by 12, with a combing 8 inches high. These hatches had hinged covers with rubber gaskets, and were bolted from the inside. In the sides and ends of these combings glasses were inserted to sight from. There was an opening made in the top of the boat for an air box, a casting with a closed top 12 by 18 by 4 inches, made to carry a hollow shaft. This shaft passed through stuffing boxes. On each end was an elbow with a 4-foot length of 1 1/2-inch pipe, and keyed to the hollow shaft; on the inside was a lever with a stop-cock to admit air.[8]

The dimensions given by Alexander are in very good agreement with those provided by an eyewitness who saw the submarine after it was moved to Charleston, Colonel Charles H. Olmstead, commanding at Fort Johnson on James Island. In his "Reminiscences of Service in Charleston Harbor in 1863," found in volume 11 (1883) of the *Southern Historical Society Papers*, Colonel Olmstead states: "This boat was one day made fast to the wharf at Fort Johnson, preparatory to an expedition against the fleet, and taking advantage of the opportunity, I examined it critically. It was built of boiler iron, about 30 feet in length, with a breadth of beam of 4 feet by a vertical depth of 6 feet, the figures being approximate only."

It has generally been reported that the *Hunley* sank and claimed its first crew while experimenting in Mobile Bay. However, neither

William Alexander nor James McClintock—the two men who should know best—mention such a sinking. General P.G.T. Beauregard, who became intimately associated with the submarine while it operated in Charleston, does not mention it, nor do any of the men who bought shares in the *Hunley.* There are no official records or writings supporting such a claim.

Furthermore, as will be described later, after the submarine tragically claimed five volunteers from the CSS *Chicora* during operations in Charleston harbor, Horace Hunley readily procured a volunteer crew from men in Mobile who had built and first operated it. If the vessel had indeed sunk and claimed its first crew in Mobile, it is doubtful Hunley would have had much success acquiring another crew from the same group of men after the submarine repeated the tragic stunt in Charleston. Of course, the second submarine—the *American Diver*—did sink in Mobile, but without loss of life. This fact may be the source of the distorted claims regarding the *Hunley* sinking in Mobile.

While the gallant submarine builders were practicing with the *Hunley* in Mobile Bay, the defenses around Charleston, South Carolina, were beginning to wither under a prolonged Federal siege. The harbor was lined with Union warships and monitors, each sending a storm of iron hail against the shore batteries and forts. The Confederates had placed rope obstructions and torpedoes in the harbor to halt the Federal advance, but General Beauregard, in charge of Charleston's defenses, desperately needed help. Consequently, General Maury offered the submarine to General Beauregard, who quickly accepted.

General Pierre Gustave Toutant Beauregard, the son of an aristocratic family of southern Louisiana, had graduated from West Point Academy in 1838. Beauregard believed in states' rights more deeply than most, and when Louisiana seceded from the Union, he resigned his post with the Federal government. It is interesting to speculate that General Beauregard may have been acquainted with Horace Hunley, as Beauregard had served in New Orleans in 1856, being in charge of army engineering works there.

On August 7, 1863, the following order concerning transporting the submarine was issued by General Beauregard: "Quartermasters and Railroad Agents on Lines from Charleston, S.C., to Mobile, Alabama: Please expedite transportation of Whitney's submarine boat from Mobile here. It is much needed."[9]

As Civil War–era rail cars were only about 20 feet long, the much longer submarine was placed on two platform cars and then shipped to Charleston.[10] Considered a secret weapon with which its designers hoped to relieve the city from its precarious predicament, the submarine was shrouded in canvas to escape prying eyes during the long rail journey. James McClintock and B. A. (Gus) Whitney apparently accompanied the vessel to Charleston.

It is interesting that Beauregard's order refers to the *Hunley* as "Whitney's submarine boat." Gus Whitney was only a part-owner of the *Hunley*, having invested in a $5,000 share with J. D. Breaman. A later communication from Thomas Jordan, General Beauregard's chief of staff, is addressed to B. A. Whitney, "in charge of submarine torpedo boat." So it appears that while McClintock was given the command of the *Hunley*, it was Whitney who received overall responsibility and supervision of the vessel's operation. By August 15 the men and their submarine had arrived in Charleston, for on that date Thomas Jordan sent the following communication to Whitney:

> I am authorized to say that John Fraser & Co. will pay over to any parties who shall destroy the U.S. steam iron-clad *Ironsides* the sum of $100,000, a similar sum for the destruction of the wooden frigate *Wabash*, and the sum of $50,000 for every monitor sunk.
>
> I have reason to believe that other men of wealth will unite and give with equal munificence toward the same end.
>
> At the same time, steps are being taken to secure a large sum to be settled for the support of the families of parties, who, making any attempt against the fleet now attacking our outworks, shall fail in the enterprise, and fall or be captured in the attempt."[11]

Hunley and his associates had apparently abandoned their plans of privateering, as no application for a letter of marque was made for either the *American Diver* or the *Hunley.* At this late date it cannot be known what, exactly, prompted Hunley to bear the financial burden

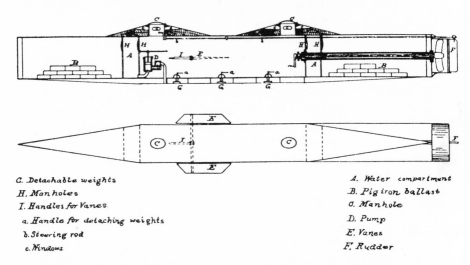

G. *Detachable weights*
H. *Man holes*
I. *Handles for Vanes*
a. *Handle for detaching weights*
b. *Steering rod*
c. *Windows*

A. *Water compartment*
B. *Pig iron ballast*
C. *Manhole*
D. *Pump*
E. *Vanes*
F. *Rudder*

This drawing of the Hunley *originally appeared in Rear Admiral G. W. Baird's article in the August 1902 issue of the* Journal of American Societies of Naval Engineers. *According to Rear Admiral Baird, the drawing was based upon figures given to him by James McClintock and sketches made in McClintock's presence. As historian Eustace Williams has pointed out, "The sweetness of the boat's lines is in sharp contrast to the blunt bow and stern of Alexander's memory of the vessel." The drawing actually appears to be a cross between the* Pioneer *and the* Hunley. *In comparison to both Alexander's drawing and the Conrad Wise Chapman painting, the dimensions are way off. The bow and stern castings appear too long and too tapered. The placement of the diving planes is wrong. No force pump is shown for the after ballast tank. Even the design and placement of the water ballast tanks is in opposition with other accounts. These are just a few of the many discrepancies. Perhaps the most telling is the propeller crank. How could the* Hunley*'s crew of eight men turn the propeller via one tiny handle?*

of the *American Diver*, or others to join him in financing the *Hunley*. Perhaps it was a strong sense of honor and loyalty to the South; perhaps it was simply desire for profit.

As members of the special engineer corps, the owners of the *Hunley* were to receive half the value of every ship they destroyed, and the generous offer from John Fraser promised additional profits for the submarine's owners. There is evidence, however, that Hunley's actions were spurred not merely by desire for profit but by an extreme loyalty to the Confederacy. Confident of the submarine's ability to surprise and destroy enemy vessels, on August 15 Hunley wrote to James McClintock of the further opportunities presented by the unique craft's presence in Charleston harbor:

> I have been extremely anxious about your experiment at Charleston. It is not at all on the question of whether you will succeed in blowing up a vessel of the enemy, for I think that more than probable and of itself only a small matter. It is whether your success will be made available in effecting a real solid benefit to the Confederacy and conferring glory on its originators.
>
> I am anxious first and above all for a dead silence on our part that the enemy may be lost in uncertainty and mystery, which is more dreadful than any understood evil even of the greatest magnitude. Secondly, while in a panic if you succeed the enemy if properly pressed before he can make preparations to resist the consequences of your success might be possibly driven entirely from Morris Island, his works destroyed and guns spiked even if it be not possible to take and permanently hold the island and prevent it from being retaken.
>
> Therefore, as I cannot join you I would be glad to have you in conversation with General Beauregard if this reaches you before your experiment to ask him (by way of suggestion) if you should be so fortunate as to succeed, and if that success should create a panic and consequent retreat, if a rapid descent by vessels and men could not drive the enemy from the island.
>
> If he should think that a panic and retreat of the enemies could effect such a result, then make every effort first to get him to prepare silently

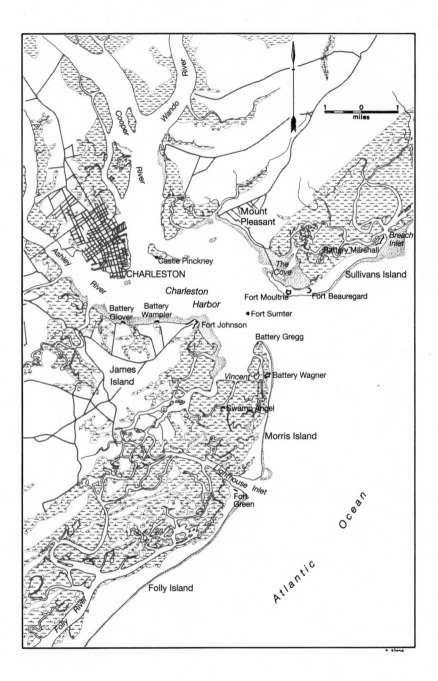

for such an event, and then by at least one spare torpedo for a second attempt make a heroic attempt to produce this panic. Remind your crew of Manassas and Shiloh and the consequences of faltering in the hour of success and make one grand effort you may have cause to rejoice over the fruits of your labor and like men in more exalted positions you did stop to rejoice over your small gains let slip a vast success and immortal honor. Read this to Whitney.[12]

To the untrained eye, Morris Island appeared a seemingly worthless piece of real estate. "It is a long, narrow strip of sand, running almost due north and south for about four miles, varying in breadth from, say one hundred yards at the narrowest point to half a mile at the broadest," wrote Colonel Olmstead. "Upon the west side the Island is separated from James Island by Vincent's Creek and by broad marshes intersected by numerous salt water creeks, while its eastern shore is washed throughout its entire length by the waters of the Atlantic Ocean. . . . The surface of the island is but little raised above the level of the sea and presents a glaring stretch of white sandy hillocks, which were sparsely dotted with the coarse grasses of the coast, and which changed their contours in every high wind."[13] To military leaders of both North and South, however, Morris Island was of vital strategic importance. This little island, vulnerable to takeover by the Federals, could open the door to Charleston.

Charleston, nestled between the Ashley and Cooper rivers, was looked upon by many a Northerner as the heart of the rebellion. It was at Charleston that the first shots of the war rang out—shots that presaged many long years of turmoil and anguish—shots that tolled the death knell for many a brave soldier. The beautiful but defiant city was despised by the Federals. By mounting guns on nearby Morris Island, the city could be demolished and her spirit broken. Charleston harbor, a major port for blockade-runners and thus an important source of raw materials for the struggling Confederacy, would also be destroyed. But there was a catch. Morris Island was armed, and taking it from the Confederates would not be an easy task. Colonel Olmstead described the island's intimidating defenses:

At the northern extremity of the island, known as Cumming's Point, was located Battery Gregg, and about 3/4 of a mile to the south of this, Battery Wagner stretched entirely across the island from the sea on the left, to Vincent's Creek on the right, the battery facing due south. It was an irregular work. On the extreme left, a heavy traverse and curtain protected the sally port and gave a flanking fire down the beach, to any force that might assail the main work. Then came a salient, one face of which commanded the ship channel, then a broken line, arranged for flanking fires, extending to the marsh. The parapets were solid, and a broad, deep, dry moat added boldness to their profile. . . . The armament consisted of one 10-inch Columbiad and some 32-pounders in the sea face, and four or five lighter guns, chiefly howitzers on the land-side.[14]

Both Morris Island and Battery Wagner were strategically located for the Confederates. The main channel by which ships entered Charleston harbor ran within easy cannon range of the battery. The channel then crossed to the north and passed between Fort Moultrie, on Sullivan's Island, and Fort Sumter, built upon a shoal midway between Sullivan's Island and Morris Island. The heavy warships and monitors comprising the Federal fleet could operate only in the deep water of the main channel. Therefore, the vessels could not come within shooting range of Fort Sumter without also coming within range of Confederate cannon located in Battery Wagner.

In addition, Confederate defenses within the harbor were not yet fully prepared to defend Charleston against a major attack. The responsibility fell on Battery Wagner to keep the main channel clear of Federal vessels and to further protect the city of Charleston. While General Beauregard realized Wagner could not hold out indefinitely, he hoped to gain the precious time required to strengthen his other defensive positions.

When Horace Hunley wrote to his compatriot James McClintock on August 15, Battery Wagner was in a grave situation. During June the Federals had secretly placed some forty-seven guns and mortars in batteries on the northern tip of Folly Island. This island lay to the south of Morris Island, just across a narrow stretch of water known as Lighthouse Inlet. With these batteries, the Federals successfully drove the Confederates from the southern portion of Morris Island on the morning of July 10 and established a base from which infantry attacks could be directed against Battery Wagner.

Strong Federal assaults immediately followed on July 11 and 18. Although Battery Wagner had repulsed these attacks, its future was extremely uncertain, as the Federals had then laid siege to the battery. Pounded almost daily by Union monitors, and being rapidly approached by a series of skillfully executed parallels, the battery threatened to fall at any moment. How long Wagner could hold out was anyone's guess. It was for this reason Hunley had written to McClintock, encouraging him to quickly attack the Federal fleet. It was Hunley's hope that through the element of surprise, the submarine might create a panic and the enemy be "driven entirely from Morris Island, his

From The Illustrated London News, December 5, 1863

An artist's rendition of shells exploding in Charleston in December, 1863.

works destroyed and guns spiked."

Two days after Hunley wrote to McClintock, a shocking event added even more to the gravity of the situation in Charleston. On August 17, the Federals began their first major bombardment of Fort Sumter. According to Colonel Olmstead:

> It had been thought that the grand old fort was safe so long as Wagner held out. But one morning a new battery opened; the shot and shell went high above our heads, and were hurled with irresistible power against the walls of Sumter. Great masses of masonry from the outer wall fell as each shot struck, and ere many days it seemed as though nought but a pile of ruins would mark the spot. . . . This bombardment lasted for seven days, and in that time a first-class masonry fort was reduced to a shapeless ruin from batteries located at points far beyond the remotest distance at which any engineer had ever dreamed of danger.[15]

Fort Sumter, a five-sided brick masonry fort whose 5-foot-thick outer walls once towered 50 feet above the water, was now little more than a shapeless mound of debris. Virtually all firepower was gone. What little remained could command the ship channel, but do absolutely nothing to support Battery Wagner on nearby Morris Island. The battery's garrison was now totally on their own. If only McClintock could create a panic with the submarine, the battery might yet be saved. But, as shall soon be demonstrated, action on the part of James McClintock was not forthcoming.

The events on Morris Island worried Charleston; the bombardment of Fort Sumter shocked Charleston; the next event would dismay her. Early on the morning of August 22, around 1:30 A.M., Charleston's residents were roused from their slumber by the awful shriek and explosion of a 150-pound incendiary bomb bursting in their city. Before dawn finally hovered on the horizon, fourteen more rounds were pumped into the very heart of the city. The "Swamp Angel" had announced its presence.

Also known as the "Marsh Battery," Swamp Angel was capable of lofting a 200-pound projectile into Charleston, some four miles away.

This monstrous 8-inch Parrott cannon weighed 16,500 pounds, and had been secretly placed by the Federals in the marsh of none other

than Morris Island. Battery Wagner was about to fall, Fort Sumter was all but destroyed, and now Swamp Angel threatened to level Charleston. Now more than ever General Beauregard needed Captain Hunley's plan to drive the Federals off Morris Island.

But something was definitely wrong. The *H. L. Hunley* was at Charleston, ready to do her greatest service for the struggling Confederacy. James McClintock and Gus Whitney were there to supervise its operation, and a handsome reward had been posted by John Fraser for the destruction of enemy vessels. The reports circulating around Charleston, however, indicated absolutely nothing was happening with the submarine. On August 23, Brigadier General T. L. Clingman, commanding on Sullivan's Island, reported to Assistant Adjutant General Captain W. F. Nance: "The torpedo-boat started out at sunset, but returned, as they state, because of an accident. *Whitney says that though McClintock is timid,* yet it shall go tonight unless the weather is bad" (italics added).[16]

McClintock did not take the submarine out that night. An additional message from Brigadier General Clingman to Captain Nance just a few hours later summed up the situation: "The torpedo boat has not gone out. *I do not think it will render any service under its present management*" (italics added).[17]

No further mention of James McClintock is made in any official records or any correspondence concerning the *Hunley.* McClintock appears to have dropped out of the *Hunley* picture entirely; how long he remained in Charleston is not even known. It is clear from McClintock's letter written to Matthew Fontaine Maury after the war that while he knew of the *Hunley's* later actions, he had no further involvement with the submarine.

General Beauregard desperately needed action on the part of the Confederate submarine *Hunley.* Therefore, it is not surprising that Beauregard would relieve the ineffective McClintock of command of the vessel. To do so, however, required Beauregard to take military possession of the *Hunley,* as she was privately owned. A letter on file at the South Carolina Library, written on August 30, 1863, by Theodore A. Honour, indicates this is precisely what happened:

You doubtless remember and perhaps you saw while in the City the iron torpedo boat which certain parties brought from Mobile to blow up the Ironsides. They have been out three times without accomplishing anything, and the government suspecting something wrong, proposed to them to allow a Naval Officer to go with them on their next trial, which they refused. *The boat was therefore seized and yesterday nine men from one of the gunboats were placed in her to learn how to work her and go out and see what they could do* (italics added).

Official correspondence from Major John F. O'Brien to Brigadier General R. S. Ripley, dated September 24, 1863, substantiates Honour's claim that the *Hunley* was seized. According to Major O'Brien: "He (General Beauregard) also directs you to appoint a board of competent persons, to estimate the value of the submarine torpedo-boat *at the time she was taken possession of by the military authorities*" (italics added).[18]

Thus it becomes apparent that General Beauregard removed James McClintock and his civilian crew from control of the *Hunley*. As McClintock's replacement, Beauregard selected Lieutenant John Payne of the Confederate States Navy, who had taken an interest in the submarine torpedo-boat. Lieutenant Payne was attached to the Confederate ram *Chicora* and volunteered with a crew of eight men, also of the *Chicora*, to launch the *Hunley* for an attack against the *New Ironsides*, what many considered to be the Goliath of the Federal fleet. On Saturday, August 29, as the submarine was being towed across Charleston harbor, disaster struck. An extract from Colonel Olmstead's daily report made the following day reads as follows: "An unfortunate accident occurred at the wharf yesterday, by which 5 seamen of the *Chicora* were drowned. The submarine torpedo boat became entangled in some way with ropes, was drawn on its side, filled, and went down. The bodies have not yet been recovered."[19]

According to a brief article in the *Charleston Daily Courier* for August 31, 1863, "Four of the men belonged to the gunboat *Chicora*, and were named Frank Doyle, John Kelly, Michael Cane, and Nicholas

Davis. The fifth man, whose name we did not learn, was attached to the *Palmetto State*." The name of this fifth brave man, who went to his death on board the submarine, has unfortunately been lost to history.

Concerning the events on that fateful August 29, Lieutenant C. L. Stanton of the *Chicora* wrote: "One day when Lieutenant Payne, my friend and shipmate, was aboard the *Chicora* I arranged to go down under the water with him; but as the boat was obliged to leave before my watch on deck was over, Lieutenant Charles H. Hasker took my place. She dived about the harbor successfully for an hour or two and finally went over to Fort Johnson, where the little steamer *Etiwan* was lying alongside the wharf."[20] Mr. Hasker related:

We were lying astern of the steamer *Etiwan*, near Fort Johnson, in Charleston harbor. Lieutenant Payne, who had charge, got fouled in the manhole by the hawser and in trying to clear himself got his foot on the lever which controlled the fins. He had just previously given the order to go ahead. The boat made a dive while the manholes were open and filled rapidly. Payne got out of the forward hole and two others out of the aft hole. Six of us went down with the boat. I had to get over the bar which connected the fins and through the manhole. This I did by forcing myself through the column of water which was rapidly filling the boat. The manhole plate came down on my back; but I worked my way out until my left leg was caught by the plate, pressing the calf of my leg in two. Held in this manner, I was carried to the bottom in 42 feet of water. When the boat touched bottom I felt the pressure relax. Stooping down, I took hold of the manhole plate, drew out my wounded limb, and swam to the surface. Five men were drowned on this occasion. . . . I was the only man that went to the bottom with the "Fish Boat" and came up to tell the tale.[21]

Many sources have claimed that the *Hunley* sank not once, but twice while under the command of Lieutenant Payne. In addition to the August 29 sinking just described, which claimed five men from the *Chicora*, a similar incident is said to have occurred one week earlier, also claiming several men from the *Chicora*. The question naturally arises as to whether Lieutenant Payne would have immediately volunteered for further action with the submarine if she had met with disaster under his command the week prior.

Furthermore, if he had met with a previous disaster, it is doubtful that Lieutenant Payne would have felt so confident of the vessel's operation that one week later he would be offering rides to others, as related by Lieutenant Stanton. Additionally, if the tiny *Hunley* had sunk around August 22, the vessel would have to be located, raised, cleaned up, and refitted . . . all of which requires time. It is unlikely that all this could have been accomplished, a second crew trained, and routine diving operations once again undertaken by August 29.

In all likelihood, both reported sinkings refer to the August 29 event. Official records prove that James McClintock was in charge of the submarine on August 23, the date around which the first disaster under Lieutenant Payne was said to have occurred. Sometime between August 23 and August 29 the ineffective McClintock was removed and Lieutenant Payne placed in command. Payne then secured a volunteer crew from the *Chicora* and began practicing with the novel vessel. The fact remains, however, that McClintock was in charge on August 23, and no sinking occurred on or around that date. Indeed, there are no official records to support a claim that the *Hunley* sank under Payne other than on August 29.

Word soon reached Hunley in Mobile that his submarine had somehow sunk in Charleston harbor and tragically claimed five lives. Trusting in the seaworthiness of the vessel, Hunley assumed that the tragedy had been caused by the naval crew's unfamiliarity with the unique craft. Hunley decided to offer his services, and wrote to General Beauregard on September 19:

> I am a part owner of the torpedo boat the *Hunley*. I have been interested in building this description of boat since the beginning of the war, and furnished the means entirely of building the predecessor of this boat, which was lost in an attempt to blow up a Federal vessel off Fort Morgan in Mobile harbor. I feel therefore a deep interest in its success. I propose

if you will place the boat in my hands to furnish a crew . . . from Mobile who are well acquainted with its management and make the attempt to destroy a vessel of the enemy as early as practicable.[22]

Although strategic Battery Wagner had been abandoned on the night of September 6, there was still a pressing need to attack Federal vessels off Charleston harbor. Hunley's offer was therefore quickly accepted, and on September 22 Beauregard's chief of staff, Thomas Jordan, issued orders to repair the vessel and prepare her once again for operations against the Federal fleet. Major I. T. Trezevant, commanding the arsenal, was requested to "have all work done for Captain Hunley that he may require with the utmost celerity and to supply such material as he will requisition . . ."[23] Brigadier General Ripley was directed to have the vessel cleaned and turned over to Hunley "with the understanding that said boat shall be ready for service in two weeks."[24] All repairs were to be made at the expense of the Confederate States.

Regarding Captain Hunley's taking a crew to Charleston to operate the submarine, William Alexander wrote the following: "General Beauregard then turned the boat over to a volunteer crew from Mobile, known as the 'Hunley and Parks crew.' Captain Hunley and Thomas Parks (one of the best of men), of the firm of Parks and Lyons, in whose shop the boat had been built, were in charge, with Messrs. Brockbank, Patterson, McHugh, Marshall, White, Beard, and another, as the crew, and until the day this crew left Mobile it was understood that the writer of this was to be one of them, but on the eve of that day Mr. Parks prevailed on the writer to let him take his place. Nearly all the men had had some experience in the boat before leaving Mobile, and were well qualified to operate her."[25]

Significantly, Alexander makes no mention of a Lieutenant Dixon going to Charleston with Captain Hunley and the rest of the crew. "Lieutenant George E. Dixon, like myself, was a mechanical engineer and belonged to the same regiment, the 21st Alabama," wrote Alexander. "He had taken great interest in the boats while building, and during their operations in Mobile River, and would have been one of the 'Hunley and Parks' crew had there been a vacancy."[26]

General Beauregard, however, clearly states that Lieutenant Dixon accompanied Hunley to Charleston, and further implies that it was Dixon who was primarily responsible for the submarine: "After the recovery of the sunken boat Mr. Hunley came from Mobile, *bringing with him Lieutenant Dixon*, of the Alabama volunteers, who had successfully experimented with the boat in the harbor of Mobile, and under him another naval crew volunteered to work it . . . *Lieutenant Dixon made repeated descents* in the harbor of Charleston, diving under the naval receiving ship which lay at anchor there" (italics added).[27]

The fact that Lieutenant Dixon went to Charleston with Thomas Parks and Captain Hunley will become even more apparent later in the chapter. It is indeed probable that Lieutenant Dixon was the "another" whom Alexander referred to. There is no apparent reason why Alexander omitted Dixon's involvement with the submarine at this time.

In any event, the *Hunley* with her experienced crew was once again proving herself in the water of Charleston harbor. Under Lieutenant Dixon's expert command, test dives were again going smoothly and General Beauregard's confidence in the boat was growing daily. Plans were no doubt being finalized for an assault against the blockading fleet when Lieutenant Dixon was unexpectedly called away from the submarine. During his absence tragedy once again struck. According to General Beauregard: "*One day when he [Lieutenant Dixon] was absent from the city Mr. Hunley, unfortunately, wishing to handle the boat himself,* made the attempt. It was readily submerged, but did not rise again to the surface, and all on board perished" (italics added).[28]

The Journal of Operations kept at the Confederate headquarters in Charleston reads for October 15, 1863: "An unfortunate accident occurred this morning with the submarine boat, by which Captain H. L. Hunley and seven men lost their lives in an attempt to run under the navy receiving ship. The boat left the wharf at 9:25 A.M. and disappeared at 9:35. As soon as she sunk air bubbles were seen to rise to the surface of the water, and from this fact it is supposed the hole in the top of the boat by which the men entered was not properly closed. It was impossible at the time to make any effort to rescue the unfortunate men, as the water was some 9 fathoms deep."[29]

The *Charleston Daily Courier* for October 16, 1863, carried the following short note: "On Thursday morning an accident occurred to a small boat in Cooper river, containing eight persons, all of whom were drowned. . . . Their bodies, we believe, have all been recovered."

The bodies of the unfortunate men had actually not been recovered. Indeed, although the sunken submarine was finally located on October 18, it was not raised until November 7, after having remained under water for some twenty-three days.

General Beauregard recorded the gruesome scene as the boat was opened: "When the boat was discovered, raised and opened, the spectacle was indescribably ghastly; the unfortunate men were contorted into all kinds of horrible attitudes; some clutching candles, evidently endeavoring to force open the man-holes; others lying in the bottom tightly grappled together, and the blackened faces of all presented the expression of their despair and agony."[30]

The pitiful remains of Horace Hunley, Thomas Parks, Robert Brockbank, Joseph Patterson, Charles McHugh, John Marshall, Henry Beard, and Charles Sprague were at last laid to rest in Charleston's Magnolia Cemetery on November 8.

The "Peripatetic Coffin," as some gloomily nicknamed her, had claimed her second crew. What had happened? Her crew was well practiced in operating the submarine, having successfully dived and surfaced the vessel many times before. What had gone awry? William Alexander offered the following explanation:

The boat, when found, was lying on the bottom at an angle of about 35 degrees, the bow deep in the mud. The holding-down bolts of each cover had been removed. When the hatch covers were lifted considerable air and gas escaped. Captain Hunley's body was forward, with his head in the forward hatchway, his right hand on top of his head (he had been trying, it would seem, to raise the hatch cover). In his left hand was a candle that had never been lighted, the sea cock on the forward end, on Hunley's ballast tank, was wide open, the cock-wrench not on the plug, but lying on the bottom of the boat. Mr. Park's body was found with his head in the after hatchway, his right hand above his head. He also had been trying to raise his hatch cover, but the pressure was too great. The sea cock to his tank was nearly empty. The other bodies were floating in the water. Hunley and Parks were undoubtedly asphyxiated, the others drowned. The bolts that held the iron keel ballast had been partially turned, but not sufficient to release it.

In the light of these conditions, we can easily depict before our minds, and almost as readily explain, what took place in the boat during the moments immediately following its submergence. Captain Hunley's practice with the boat had made him quite familiar and expert in handling her, and this familiarity produced at this time forgetfulness. It was found in practice to be easier on the crew to come to the surface by giving the pumps a few strokes and ejecting some of the water ballast, than by the momentum of the boat operating on the elevated fins. At this time the boat was under way, lighted through the dead-lights in the hatchways. He partly turned the fins to go down, but thought, no doubt, that he needed more ballast and opened his sea cock. Immediately the boat was in total darkness. He then undertook to light the candle. While trying to do this the tank quickly flooded, and under great pressure the boat sank very fast and soon overflowed, and the first intimation they would have of anything being wrong was the water rising fast, but noiselessly, about their feet in the bottom of the boat. They tried to release the iron keel ballast, but did not turn the keys quite far enough, therefore failed. The water soon forced the air to the top of the boat and into the hatchways, where Captains Hunley and Parks were found. Parks had pumped his ballast tank dry, and no doubt Captain Hunley had exhausted himself on his pump, but he had forgotten that he had not closed his sea-cock.[31]

Alexander's explanation of the *Hunley's* loss, while possible, is based largely upon his assumption that "Captain Hunley's practice with the boat had made him quite familiar and expert in handling her, and this familiarity produced forgetfulness." However, Alexander was in Mobile, not Charleston, at that time and could not possibly have known to what extent Hunley had practiced with the submarine. It is more likely that rather than Hunley's familiarity with the submarine, it was his unfamiliarity and lack of experience that precipitated the disaster.

According to General Beauregard, Lieutenant Dixon had accompanied Hunley to Charleston, and *"Lieutenant Dixon* made repeated descents in the harbor of Charleston" (italics added). Significantly, General Beauregard placed the emphasis of the submarine's operations upon Lieutenant Dixon, not Captain Hunley. Further, General Beauregard, in referring to the day the submarine sank, stated: "But, one day when he [Lieutenant Dixon] was absent from the city, Mr. Hunley, unfortunately, wishing to handle the boat himself, made the attempt." Beauregard's statements definitely convey the impression that it was Dixon who was familiar with the vessel, and that Captain Hunley lacked experience.

Although William Alexander fails to place Lieutenant Dixon in Charleston at the time, it is obvious for the following reasons that Dixon was indeed there with Captain Hunley. First, General Beauregard's previous statements claimed Dixon accompanied Hunley to Charleston and practiced with the submarine. Second, the bodies of only eight men were recovered from the wreck: the submarine was designed to operate with a full complement of nine men. It is probable that the ninth man was an absent Lieutenant Dixon. Why would they operate, otherwise, short-handed? If the vacant ninth position did belong to Dixon, where was he?

First Assistant Engineer James H. Tomb may provide the answer. According to Tomb: "At the time she made the attempt to dive under the receiving ship in Charleston Harbor, *Lieutenant Dixon, James Eason, and myself stood on the wharf as she passed out* and saw her dive, but she did not rise again" (italics added).[32] This is the last piece of evidence placing Lieutenant Dixon in Charleston, but not within the submarine, during the fateful dive on October 15, 1863.

Apparently it was Dixon who was well versed in the operation of the submarine. It was during Dixon's absence, while Captain Hunley was commanding, that problems developed. There is further evidence to indicate the problems were caused by an *inexperienced* Captain Hunley at the controls. Looking again at Alexander's description of the vessel when recovered, the following points stand out. First, the submarine was stuck fast in the mud at a dive angle of 35 degrees. Second, Hunley's sea-cock was open and the vessel was flooded. Third, Captain Hunley's candle had never been lighted.

It was normal practice in operating the submarine to bring the vessel to "diving trim" before executing a dive. The sequence of events would be roughly as follows: With both hatches securely fastened down, the commander would light his candle. This candle served the dual purpose of alerting the crew when oxygen was running low, as well as illuminating the crude compass, depth gauge, steering wheel, and diving lever. Water ballast would then be admitted to the forward and after ballast tanks until the top of the hull lay about 3 inches below the surface of the water. The sea-cocks would then be closed, and with the propeller

Courtesy of the National Archives

One of several steam-powered Confederate torpedo boats built on the model of the David *and privately financed in Charleston.*

turning, the diving lever would be gently depressed until the vessel was pulled down to the desired depth. Perhaps the following scenario, based on this information, is a more realistic theory of what transpired on board the *Hunley* shortly before the tragic accident. As the vessel cast off from the wharf, Horace Hunley opened the sea-cock to the forward tank while Thomas Parks opened the valve to the after tank. Significantly, Hunley had failed to light his candle. As the vessel reached diving trim, Parks closed his sea-cock, but the inexperienced Hunley forgot to close his. With water still flooding into the forward tank, Hunley depressed the diving lever, perhaps too far or too fast. Plunged into darkness, the little submarine went into a steep 35-degree dive.

In the brief period that followed, Hunley may have been attempting to light his candle, or perhaps he was groping in the dark for the wrench to his sea-cock. Whatever his actions, the submarine promptly buried her bow in the muddy bottom of Charleston harbor, hopelessly stuck. Unable to back her out of the sticky mud, the crew's only hope lay in releasing the auxiliary ballast and buoying to the surface.

But time was quickly running out. Water was spilling over the top of Hunley's tank and filling the submarine. The men clawed frantically at the bolts holding the keel ballast, but drowned in the rapidly rising water before the weights could be fully detached. Hunley and Parks violently worked their force pumps, but the water kept rising. The two men released the bolts securing the hatch covers in a last desperate attempt to escape their iron coffin. But it was to no avail. The overbearing pressure of the water above prevented the covers from lifting. The air, what little remained, soon turned stale. Together in the darkness at the bottom of Charleston harbor, the two awaited the inescapable end . . . which soon arrived.

After the tragedy that claimed Captain Hunley and his entire crew, General Beauregard at first refused to allow the submarine to be used again. "But Lieutenant Dixon, a brave and determined man, having returned to Charleston," wrote Beauregard, "applied to me for authority to use it against the Federal steam sloop-of-war *Housatonic*, a powerful new vessel, carrying eleven guns of the largest caliber, which lay at the time in the north channel, opposite Breach Inlet, materially obstructing the passage of our blockade runners in and out. At the suggestion of my chief of staff, General Jordan, I consented to its use for this purpose, not as a submarine machine, but in the same manner as the *David.*"[33]

The *David* was a cigar-shaped wooden vessel designed by two Charleston men, Theodore D. Stoney and Dr. St. Julian Ravenal. Built in 1863, the steam-propelled launch measured nearly 50 feet long with a 6-foot beam. Ballasted to sit low in the water, the *David* carried a spar torpedo projecting from its bow. On the night of October 5, 1863, the *David*, commanded by Lieutenant W. T. Glassel, made a daring attack upon the Union warship *New Ironsides.* Under cover of darkness, Lieutenant Glassel successfully approached the *New Ironsides* and rammed his spar torpedo against its iron-plated hull. Due to delayed fuse action, the torpedo bounced off the hull before detonating under the vessel's starboard quarter.

The explosion rocked the huge warship, and threw up a geyser that sent water down the *David's* small stack, nearly extinguishing its fires. Without power and under a barrage of gunfire, Lieutenant Glassel

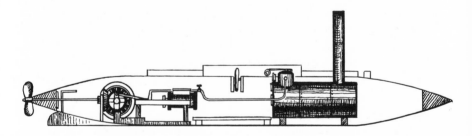

On the night of October 5, 1863, the warship New Ironsides *was rocked by the explosion of a torpedo delivered by the Confederate torpedo boat* David. *The attack created a flurry of excitement in the South which led to the construction of a number of* Davids *during the remainder of the war. Protected by a thin layer of iron, these steam-propelled vessels were approximately 50 feet long with a 6-foot beam.*

ordered his three-man crew to abandon ship. Lifeless, the *David* slowly drifted away from the stricken warship. Lieutenant Glassel and his fireman were soon captured by the Federals. Engineer James H. Tomb swam back to the disabled torpedo boat, where he found the pilot clinging to the vessel's side. The two men were able to restore the *David*'s fires and cautiously make their way back to port. Severely shaken by the blast, the *New Ironsides* was later sent north for repairs.

After securing another crew of volunteers from the *Indian Chief*, Lieutenant Dixon and his new assistant, William Alexander, once again began practicing with the boat in Charleston harbor. Despite General Beauregard's intent that the *Hunley* only be used as a surface craft, it is clear that Dixon actually continued to dive with the submarine. A Mr. Belton, whose first name has been lost to history, deserted from the Confederate Navy and reported what he knew of the *Hunley* to the Federal authorities on January 7, 1864.

Belton had worked as an engineer on the railroad between Montgomery and Mobile, and was familiar with the *Hunley* because he had sometimes worked near the shop in Mobile where the submarine was being built. While working on the railroad he was conscripted into the Confederate Navy. He arrived in Charleston on October 24, 1863, and was sent on board the *Indian Chief.* According to Belton's examination:

> Saw her when she was raised the last time. They then hoisted her out of the water, refitted her, and got another crew. *Saw her after that submerged.* Saw her go under the *Indian Chief,* and then saw her go back under again. She made about one-half mile in the dives. Saw her dive under the *Charleston;* went under about 250 feet from her, and came up about 300 feet beyond her. Was about twenty minutes under the water when she went under the *Indian Chief* (italics added).[34]

Belton had arrived in Charleston little more than a week after the tragic drowning of Captain Hunley and his crew. The submarine lay on the bottom of Charleston harbor until it was recovered on November 7 and once again placed in the hands of Lieutenant Dixon. While

General Beauregard had consented to its use "not as a submarine . . . but in the same manner as the *David*," Belton's statements indicate that the *Hunley* actually continued to routinely dive about the harbor.

Lieutenant Dixon and William Alexander were instructed to moor the submarine off Battery Marshall, on Sullivan's Island. They were given quarters at Mount Pleasant, some seven long miles away. That the *Hunley* and its crew were now operating under direct orders is evidenced by Beauregard's Special Orders Number 271 issued December 14, 1863:

> First Lieutenant George E. Dixon, Twenty-first Regiment Alabama Volunteers, will take command and direction of the submarine torpedo boat *H. L. Hunley*, and proceed tonight to the mouth of the harbor, or as far as capacity of the vessel will allow, and will sink and destroy any vessel of the enemy with which he can come in conflict.
>
> All officers of the Confederate army in this department are commanded, and all naval officers are requested, to give such assistance to Lieutenant Dixon in the discharge of his duties as may be practicable, should he apply therefore.[35]

Although the submarine was indeed prowling about the waters off Charleston harbor during December and January, no serious attempts were made at that time to attack an enemy vessel. After the *David*'s nearly successful attack against the *New Ironsides*, Rear Admiral John A. Dahlgren took further precautions to guard his Union vessels from the Confederates' dangerous torpedo boats. As Alexander related, "On account of chain booms having been put around the ironsides and monitors in Charleston harbor to keep us off these vessels, we had to turn our attention to the fleet outside."[36]

But the unprotected vessels in the outer harbor lay at least five miles away—much farther than the *Hunley* had traveled during its routine practice dives. No doubt Dixon spent December and much of January practicing his crew, building their stamina for the difficult and strenuous mission ahead.

Some writers have claimed that yet another sinking of the *Hunley* occurred on or around January 18. According to these sources, a Mr. Culbertson and a Mr. Yates were in charge of the submarine; the vessel experienced an erratic dive, and the entire crew lost their lives through either drowning or suffocation. However, there is no corroborating evidence to support these claims. Indeed, it is unlikely that Culbertson and Yates were ever in charge of the *Hunley.* General Beauregard clearly placed Lieutenant Dixon in command of the vessel when he issued Special Orders Number 271. After the accident that claimed Captain Hunley and his crew while Dixon was absent, it is extremely doubtful that Dixon would have allowed the submarine to make a dive without his presence on board. And what about Alexander? Where was he? For the submarine to have dived with the two most practiced and knowledgeable men absent is unlikely.

Neither William Alexander or General Beauregard—both men intimately associated with the submarine's operations in Charleston harbor—mention such a sinking with attendant loss of life. Additionally, James McClintock implied the submarine sank a total of only three times, the last occurring during the *Housatonic* attack:

This boat was taken to Charleston, and although she proved fatal to a number of people, it was from no fault of the boat or machinery; but for want of sufficient knowledge of those in charge of the boat.

The boat and machinery was so very simple, many people at the first inspection believed they could work the boat without practice or experience. Although I endeavored to prevent inexperienced people from going under water in the boat, I was not always successful. I was at all times willing to instruct any person who wished it, to tell them and show them the difficulties, which in my own mind was want of speed or power.

I never considered there would be any difficulty in going out and in destroying a vessel, but the power was not sufficient to bring the boat back to the place where she started from. The proof of which was proved in her destroying the sloop-of-war *Housatonic* blockading off the harbor of Charleston. In that case they did not work the torpedo as was contemplated by me. *In both the other cases where life was lost,* the people did not understand the management of the boat, and were in her without my knowledge or consent (italics added).[37]

Mr. J. D. Breaman, one of the *Hunley's* owners, also claimed the vessel sank only three times:

Since we have been on this side of the river we have gotten up a great many projects and have been interested in many new schemes, the particulars of which are too lengthy for an ordinary letter. Among the number, however, was a submarine boat, built at this place, of which Whitney and myself bought one-fifth for $3,000. We took her to Charleston, for the purpose of operating there, and a few days after her arrival there, she sunk through carelessness and her crew of 5 men drowned. Another crew of 8 men went on from here, raised her, and while experimenting with her in the harbor, sunk her and all 8 were drowned. Lieutenant Dixon then went on from here and got another crew in Charleston. A few nights ago he went out, attacked and sunk the steam sloop of war *Housatonic,* but, unfortunately . . . fear that he and his crew were all lost. I enclose a slip from our paper, giving an account of the affair, which will be interesting to you, as Singer and myself built the torpedoes with which the ship was destroyed, and besides we own a considerable interest in the value of the ship, as the owners and crew of the boat got one-half of her value for destroying her.[38]

Both the official records and first-hand evidence support the claim that the *Hunley* sank a total of three times. The first accident occurred on August 29, 1863, under the command of Lieutenant Payne, claiming five lives. The second disaster occurred on October 15, 1863, claiming Captain Hunley and his crew of seven men. The third and last sinking occurred shortly after the attack upon the *Housatonic* on February 17, 1864, claiming Lieutenant Dixon and his entire crew. A complete discussion of this final sinking will be given in chapter 4. But, to return to the *Hunley's* operations, Alexander left the following detailed account:

Two men experienced in handling the boat, and seven others composed the crew. The first officer steered and handled the boat forward, and the second attended to the after-tank and pumps and the air supply, all hands turning on the cranks except the first officer. There was just sufficient room for these two to stand in their places with their heads in the hatchways and take observations through the lights of the combings.

All hands aboard and ready, they would fasten the hatch covers down tight, light a candle, then let the water in from the sea into the ballast tanks until the top of the shell was about 3 inches under water. This could be seen by the water level showing through the glasses in the hatch combings. The sea cocks were then closed and the boat put under way. The captain would then lower the lever and depress the forward end of the fins very slightly, noting on the mercury gauge the depth of the boat beneath the surface; then bring the fins to a level; the boat would remain and travel at that depth. To rise to a higher level in the water he would raise the lever and elevate the forward end of the fins, and the boat would rise to its original position in the water.

If the boat was not under way, in order to rise to the surface, it was necessary to start the pumps, and lighten the boat by ejecting the water from the tanks into the sea. In making a landing, the second officer would open his hatch cover, climb out and pass a line to shore . . .

In comparatively smooth water and light current the *Hunley* could make 4 miles an hour, but in rough water the speed was much slower. It was winter, therefore necessary that we go out with the ebb and come in with the flood tide, a fair wind, and dark moon. This latter was essential to our success, as our experience had fully demonstrated the necessity of occasionally coming to the surface, slightly lifting the hatch-cover, and letting in a little air. On several occasions we came to the surface for air, opened the cover, and heard the men in the Federal picket boats talking and singing. Our daily routine, whenever possible, was about as follows:

Leave Mount Pleasant about 1 P.M., walk 7 miles to Battery Marshall on the beach (this exposed us to fire, but it was the best walking), take the boat out and practice the crew for two hours in the Back Bay. Dixon and myself would then stretch out on the beach with the compass between us and get the bearings of the nearest vessel as she took her position for the night; ship up the torpedo on the boom, and, when dark, go out, steering for the vessel, proceed until the condition of the men, sea, tide, wind, moon, and daylight compelled our return to the dock; unship the torpedo, put it under guard at Battery Marshall, walk back to quarters at Mount Pleasant, and cook breakfast.

During the months of November and December, 1863, through January and the early part of February, 1864, the wind held contrary, making it difficult, with our limited power, to make much headway. During this time we went out on an average of four nights a week, but on account of the weather, and considering the physical condition of the men to propel the boat back again, often, after going out six or seven miles, we would have to return. This we always found a task, and many times it taxed our utmost exertions to keep from drifting out to sea, daylight often breaking while we were yet in range. This experience, also our desire to know, in case we struck a vessel (circumstances required our keeping below the surface), suggested that while in safe water we make the experiment to find out how long it was possible to stay under water without coming to the surface for air and not injure the crew.

It was agreed by all hands, to sink and let the boat rest on the bottom, in the Back Bay, off Battery Marshall, each man to make equal physical exertion in turning the propeller. It was also agreed that if any one in the boat felt that he must come to the surface for air, and he gave the word 'up,' we would at once bring the boat to the surface.

It was usual, when practicing in the bay, that the banks would be lined with soldiers. One evening, after alternately diving and rising many times, Dixon and myself and several of the crew compared watches, noted the time and sank for the test. In 25 minutes after I had closed the after manhead and excluded the outer air the candle would not burn. Dixon forward and myself aft, turned on the propeller cranks as hard as we could. In comparing our individual experience afterwards, the experience of one was found to have been the experience of all. Each man had determined that he would not be the first to say 'up.' Not a word was said, except the occasional, 'How is it,' between Dixon and myself, until it was the voice of one man, the word 'up' came from all nine. We started the pumps, but I soon realized that my pump was not throwing. From experience I guessed the cause of the failure, took off the cap of the pump, lifted the valve, and drew out some seaweed that had choked it. During the time it took to do this the boat was considerably by the stern. Thick darkness prevailed. All hands had already endured what they thought was the utmost limit. Some of the crew almost lost control of themselves. It was a terrible few minutes, 'better imagined than described.' We soon had the boat to the surface and the manhead opened. Fresh air! What an experience! Well, the sun was shining when we went down, the beach lined with soldiers. It was now quite dark, with one solitary soldier gazing on the spot where he had seen the boat before going down the last time. He did not see the boat until he saw me standing on the hatch combing, calling to him to stand by to take the line. A light was struck and the time taken. We had been on the bottom 2 hours and 35 minutes. The candle ceased to burn in 25 minutes after we went down, showing that we had remained under water 2 hours and 10 minutes after the candle went out.

The soldier informed us that we had been given up for lost, that a message had been sent to General Beauregard at Charleston that the torpedo boat had been lost that evening off Battery Marshall with all hands.

We got back to the quarters at Mount Pleasant that night, went over early next morning to the city (Charleston) and reported to General Beauregard the facts of the affair. They were all glad to see us.

After making a full report of our experience, General Rains, of General Beauregard's staff, who was present, expressed some doubt of our having stayed under water two hours and ten minutes after the candle went out. Not that any of us wanted to go through the same experience again, but we did our best to get him to come over to Sullivan's Island and witness a demonstration of the fact, but without avail.[39]

While General Rains and perhaps others were reluctant to accept the crew's astonishing claim to having remained entirely submerged for nearly two and a half hours, an interesting experiment performed by Simon Lake lends credibility to Alexander's account. Around the turn of the century Mr. Lake, an early experimenter with the submarine *Argonaut*, attempted to resolve the question of air supply on board submarines.[40] Normal respiratory functions of the crew would obviously consume oxygen and produce carbon dioxide. At that time, many authorities believed it was possible to remain submerged only a short time without restoring precious oxygen to the air supply and removing the unwanted carbon dioxide. But how short a time?

Mr. Lake felt it was "essential to find out how little air a man could live on without suffering ill effects." Consequently, he constructed an airtight chamber containing 27 cubic feet of air. Into this novel chamber Lake climbed, and the door was sealed behind him. Lake waited patiently within the narrow confines of the test chamber. After forty-five minutes he noted that "matches burned brilliantly at the top but went out when lowered to waist level." The division between the air still containing life-sustaining oxygen and the air laden with the heavier carbon dioxide appeared very distinct. This indicated to Lake that fully one-half of the available oxygen had already been consumed. Based on his experiment, Lake concluded that approximately 15 to 20 cubic feet of normal air per person for each hour of submerged operation would prove sufficient.

Using the above values derived by Lake and the *Hunley*'s dimensions as given by Alexander, calculations reveal the *H. L. Hunley* could have remained entirely submerged for approximately two to two and one-half hours with no danger of asphyxiating its crew of nine men. This value is in extremely good agreement with William Alexander's claim.

Simon Lake's crude breathing experiment actually establishes a low limit to the length of time the submarine could have remained submerged. Modern textbook values are somewhat more generous, yielding values in the neighborhood of three to three and one-half hours. However, increased heart rate, shortness of breath, and other physical discomfort due to oxygen deprivation would have appeared during the dive before even two hours had elapsed. It is a tribute to these men that they remained submerged as long as they did.

Some writers have insisted that Lieutenant Dixon and his men believed that when they made an attack with the submarine they would no doubt be going to their deaths. However, the records of William

Alexander and General Beauregard contain no hint of this "doomed to die" attitude. To be sure, the *Hunley* had heretofore met with two disastrous accidents, but both of these had been caused by human error, not an inherent flaw in the vessel. The mission ahead was an extremely dangerous one, but it was not a *suicide* mission. Dixon and his men had practiced long and hard to ensure their own safety during the forthcoming attack. While each and every man was understandably concerned about his own fate, it is unlikely that a single man was so fatalistic as to believe he would not return from the mission. As a final point, the following letter written by Dixon scarcely two weeks before the epic-making attack upon the *Housatonic* certainly does not appear to come from a man who believed he was destined to die on board the *Hunley:*

. . . You stated my presence was very much needed on your little island. I have no doubt it is, but when it will get there is far more than I am able to tell at present, for beyond a doubt I am fastened to Charleston and its approaches until I am able to blow up some of their Yankee ships. If I wanted to leave here I could not do it, and I doubt very much if an order from General Maury would have any effect towards bringing me back.

I have been here over three months, have worked very hard, in fact I am working all the time. My headquarters are on Sullivan Island, and a more uncomfortable place could not be found in the Confederacy. You spoke of being on the front and holding the post of honor. Now, John, make one trip to the besieged city of Charleston and your post of honor and all danger that threatens Mobile will fade away. For the last six weeks I have not been out of the range of shells and often I am forced to go within very close proximity of the Yankee battery.

I do not want you and all of the company to think that because I am absent from them that mine is any pleasant duty or that I am absent from them because I believe there is any post of honor or fame where there is any danger, I think it must be at Charleston, for if you wish to see war every day and night, this is the place to see it.

Charleston and its defenders will occupy the most conspicuous place in the history of the war, and it shall be as much glory as I shall wish if

I can inscribe myself as one of its defenders. My duty here is more arduous than that of any officer of the 21st Alabama. Simply because I am not present to fulfill the duties of a lieutenant there are many that have formed the opinion that I am doing nothing; but I say that I have done more already than any of the 21st Alabama and I stand ready to prove my assertion by the best and highest military authority. What more I may do time alone will tell. . . .[41]

On February 5, the same day Dixon wrote the foregoing letter, Alexander received new orders from General Thomas Jordan, Beauregard's chief of staff. Alexander was to return immediately to Mobile where he was to build a breech-loading repeating gun. "This was a terrible blow," wrote Alexander, "both to Dixon and myself, after we had gone through so much together."[42] General Jordan reportedly told Alexander that he would find someone from the German artillery to take his place, but that Alexander was desperately needed in Mobile. Consequently, Alexander left Charleston—and the submarine torpedo boat *Hunley*—that night.

Lieutenant Dixon waited impatiently for a change in the weather so he could attack the Federal blockading fleet. Meanwhile, he continued to drill his crew in the submarine's operation. The crew now consisted of James A. Wicks, Arnold Becker, Fred Collins, C. Simpkins, and ——— Ridgeway (all of the Confederate Navy); C. F. Carlson (of F. W. Wagener's Company of Artillery—apparently Alexander's replacement); and probably a man named White and another named Miller (the official records are unfortunately incomplete). On February 17, nearly two weeks after Alexander's departure, the *Hunley*—with its well-practiced crew rounding to on the propeller shaft—propelled its way into history. Borne by the dying outward tide, the little submarine quietly made its way toward the unsuspecting *Housatonic*.

3

The Sinking of the USS *Housatonic*

I have respectfully to report that a boat belonging to the
Housatonic reached this ship last night at about 9:20,
giving me information that that vessel had been sunk at
8:45 P.M. by a rebel torpedo craft.

I immediately slipped our cable and started for her
anchorage, and on arriving near it, at 9:35, discovered her
sunk with her hammock nettings under water; dispatched
all boats and rescued from the wreck 21 officers and 129
men.

—Captain Joseph F. Green

The attack upon the USS *Housatonic* by the CSS *Hunley* is one of
the most remarkable events in naval history. The sinking of the
Housatonic stunned the North, and it gave the South renewed hopes
of lifting the terrible blockade that was strangling Southern ports. If
only the blockade could be lifted, the South reasoned, the bitter war
would soon sweep to a successful end. Although the *Hunley*'s attack
did not lift the Federal blockade nor materially affect the outcome of
the war in any way, the attack was nevertheless historically noteworthy.
Never before in history had an enemy vessel been sunk by a submarine,
and this incredible feat was not to be repeated until World War I, fifty
years later.

As is the case with so many other important events that occurred

59

during the Civil War, many aspects of the *Hunley*'s attack upon the *Housatonic* are veiled in mystery. Unfortunately, many of the Confederate records pertaining to the *Hunley* have been lost or destroyed. Those few documents that remain, particularly those relating directly to the *Hunley*'s attack, shed but little light on the subject.

The Federal records, while considerably more extensive than their Southern counterparts, are plagued by a problem equally frustrating to the historian. For the most part, when the Federal authorities referred to the submarine, they were dealing with an "unknown"—a secret weapon constructed by the Confederacy. While Admiral Dahlgren and others had received allegedly accurate and reliable reports regarding the submarine from Union spies and Confederate deserters, these accounts oftentimes contained erroneous or misleading information. These reports actually served little more than to alert the Federals to the existence of a strange underwater vessel that the blockading fleet should somehow be guarded against. The true operation of the unique little craft, its range, and its method of torpedo delivery were largely unknown.

By far the richest source of information pertaining to the *Hunley*'s attack is the *Proceedings of the Naval Court of Inquiry*, the court having been convened on February 26, 1864, to investigate the sinking of the *Housatonic*. Ordered by Rear Admiral John A. Dahlgren, commander of the South Atlantic Blockading Squadron, the court consisted of Captain Joseph F. Green, Captain John De Camp, and Lieutenant Commander J. C. Williamson. Lieutenant Jason B. Young of the Marine Corps served as judge advocate.

The *Proceedings*, on file in the National Archives, provides fascinating reading for the *Hunley* historian. Contained within the 105 handwritten pages is virtually all that is reliably known regarding the attack upon the *Housatonic*. Surprisingly, much of the content has been overlooked by writers and historians during the past century. Delving deeper into this remarkable document produces testimony pertinent to the mysteries surrounding history's first successful submarine attack.

A word of caution is in order, however. For the first time in naval history, the court was dealing with a totally new weapon of warfare, the submarine. The court's uncertainty in dealing with this new and unfamiliar weapon was reflected in the questions asked, but even more often in the questions that were not asked. While the court's attempt to establish the facts surrounding the *Housatonic*'s disaster was admirable, the task was an impossible one at that time. Consequently, the court was extremely careful not to assign blame to any of the ship's officers or crew. The conclusions reached by this Naval Court of Inquiry follow.

First.   That the USS *Housatonic* was blown up and sunk by a rebel torpedo craft on the night of February 17 last, about 9 o'clock P.M., while lying at an anchor in 27 feet of water off Charleston, S.C., bearing east-southeast, and distant from Fort Sumter about 5 1/2 miles. The weather at the time of the occurrence was clear, the night bright and moonlight, wind moderate from the northward and westward, sea smooth and tide half ebb, the ship's head about west-northwest.

Second.   That between 8:45 and 9 o'clock P.M. on said night an object in the water was discovered almost simultaneously by the officer of the deck and the lookout stationed at the starboard cathead, on the starboard bow of the ship, about 75 or 100 yards distant, having the appearance of a log. That on further and closer observation it presented a suspicious appearance, moved apparently with a speed of 3 or 4 knots in the direction of the starboard quarter of the ship, exhibiting two protuberances above and making a slight ripple in the water.

Third.   That the strange object approached the ship with a rapidity precluding a gun of the battery being brought to bear upon it, and finally came in contact with the ship on her starboard quarter.

Fourth.   That about 1 1/2 minutes after the first discovery of the strange object the crew were called to quarters, the cable slipped, and the engine backed.

Fifth.   That an explosion occurred about 3 minutes after the first discovery of the object, which blew up the after part of the ship, causing her to sink immediately after to the bottom, with her spar deck submerged.

Sixth.   That several shots from small arms were fired at the object while it was alongside or near the ship before the explosion occurred.

Seventh. That the watch on deck, ship, and ship's battery were in all respects prepared for a sudden offensive or defensive movement: that the lookouts were properly stationed and vigilance observed, and that officers and crew promptly assembled at their quarters.

Eighth. That order was preserved on board, and orders promptly obeyed by officers and crew up to the time of the sinking of the ship.

In view of the above facts the court have to express the opinion that no further military proceedings are necessary.

While most writers and historians have apparently accepted the Court of Inquiry's conclusions as unequivocal facts, thorough study of the *Proceedings of the Naval Court of Inquiry* makes it obvious that many of the court's findings are indeed questionable. For example, in reference to the court's second point, it seems the object was not really discovered "almost simultaneously" by the officer of the deck and the lookout on the starboard cathead. Actually, the lookout sighted the object several minutes prior to the officer's independent discovery. These precious minutes were unfortunately lost; in that lost time the *Housatonic* could possibly have escaped its attacker and doom.

Regarding the court's third point, had the "strange object" been properly reported when first discovered, the *Housatonic* could, in fact, have brought a gun to bear against its attacker, perhaps preventing the attack, and perhaps even destroying the *Hunley.*

Finally, the third and sixth points deduced by the court, taken together, imply that the torpedo exploded when the strange object came in contact with the ship. This further implies, and undoubtedly is the source for later writers' claims, that the *Hunley*—either disabled due to its proximity to the explosion, or jammed in the gaping hole produced by the explosion—sank along with the *Housatonic.* However, there is evidence that the explosion occurred only after the submarine had backed away, and that the *Hunley* did not, in fact, sink alongside its victim.

When did the torpedo detonate and what was the manner of delivery? Where was the *Hunley* when the torpedo exploded? Did the *Hunley* sink with the *Housatonic?* A complete discussion of these three questions will be left to the next chapter. Could the sinking of the *Housatonic* have been prevented by its officers and crew? Could the *Hunley* have been destroyed instead? These two questions will be discussed in the remainder of this chapter.

After days of testimony and much deliberation, the court concluded that "an object in the water was discovered almost simultaneously by the officer of the deck and the lookout stationed at the starboard cathead ... the strange object approached the ship with a rapidity precluding a gun of the battery being brought to bear upon it." However, these conclusions are not fully justified by the available evidence.

On Wednesday evening, February 17, 1864, the *Housatonic* lay quietly at anchor outside Charleston harbor, two and one-half miles from the battery on Breach Inlet, Sullivan's Island. Built at Boston in 1861, the *Housatonic* displaced 1240 tons and measured 207 feet from bow to stern. It possessed a powerful steam engine, and carried thirteen guns of medium to large caliber.

The ship was secured for the night and faced Fort Sumter, which was about six miles to the west-northwest. By all accounts, the weather was clear and pleasant. A gentle breeze blew from the northwest as the tide slowly set to the northeast. The sea, visible in the waxing moonlight, was smooth. On board the *Housatonic*, all appeared calm and peaceful.

But appearances can be misleading. In reality, the USS *Housatonic* was prepared, at a moment's notice, to take immediate offensive or defensive action. It was prepared to run down any blockade runner daring enough to make the attempt. It was prepared to battle a Confederate ram or warship the moment the enemy was seen. And it was prepared to defend itself against one of those dreaded Rebel torpedo boats, should one venture this far out in the harbor.

Memories of the *David*'s daring attack upon the *Ironsides* were fresh in the minds of Union sailors. The thought of what damage such torpedo boats were capable of inflicting was unsettling: a small pointed vessel slung low in the water, rushing out of the darkness like some form of sea monster, striking a ship and sinking it, then quickly fading back into the darkness from whence it came. Was it truly possible to defend a ship against such an infernal machine? To add to the sailors' apprehension, rumors were afloat that the Confederates possessed another type of torpedo boat, one that could operate totally submerged and therefore go quite undetected.

Indeed, accounts concerning Confederate diving torpedo boats had been circulating for several years. Perhaps the earliest official communication regarding this menace and an effective means of defending against it was written by Flag-Officer L. M. Goldsborough, commanding the North Atlantic Blockading Squadron. On October 27, 1861, Goldsborough wrote to Commander William Smith of the USS

While stationed at Charleston in 1863, Conrad Wise Chapman recorded many of the scenes around the harbor. This painting of the CSS Hunley *was dated December 6, 1863.*

Congress:

> Be on the alert for submarine infernal machines. The insurgents at Norfolk are said to possess one calculated to be used under water, and thus to attach a torpedo with a time fuze to a ship's bottom. It is, I understand, to be first towed tolerably near a ship by means of a tug, or else by boats with muffled oars, then to be submerged and so navigated to the vessel against which it is to operate.
>
> Might not a large and strong netting of rope, weighted at the bottom to go well down under water, and having tricing lines from its corners, etc., leading forward be rigged to advantage over a ship's bows at night?[1]

Flag-Officer Goldsborough's warning was heeded, and proper precautions taken, as can be seen from Commander Smith's reply, dated November 4, 1861:

> We have made with spars a frame in the shape of the letter A, which is suspended by the crosspiece from the bowsprit cap; the ends reach aft to the lower booms, resting on the water, and are secured by tackles to the ship's sides to steady them. . . . Suspended from the jibboom and under the above frame is a spar athwartships, some 30 feet long, to which is attached on its whole length a strong netting 14 feet deep and kept in a vertical position by weights at the bottom.
>
> Should such a machine . . . approach us and come near the cable, it must be caught in the net and held there until we relieve it. Or should it pass outside the net, the tube which floats on the surface to supply the inmates with fresh air would be caught on the A spars, and the supply of fresh air be cut off, causing suffocation, and if it should pass outside of the spars it would go entirely clear of the ship, doing no harm.[2]

On February 24, 1863, a little more than a year after the foregoing communication, word reached Federal authorities of a submarine prowling about Mobile Bay. James Carr, a deserter from the Confederate gunboat *Selma*, related the following to Commodore R. B. Hitchcock:

On or about the 14, an infernal machine, consisting of a submarine boat, propelled by a screw which is turned by hand, capable of holding 5 persons, and having a torpedo which was to be attached to the bottom of a vessel and exploded by means of clockwork, left Fort Morgan at 8 P.M. in charge of the Frenchman who invented it. The intention was to come up at Sand Island, get the bearing and distance of the nearest vessel, dive under again and operate upon her; but on emerging they found themselves so far outside of the island and in so strong a current (setting out) that they were forced to cut the torpedo adrift and make the best of their way back. The attempt will be renewed as early as possible, and three or four others are being constructed for the purpose.[3]

Two months later, General Hurlbut of the U.S. Army informed the secretary of war that "a submarine torpedo boat is in the course of preparation for attack upon our fleet at Mobile. . . . She will drop down close to the vessel . . . sink beneath the surface, work the propeller by hand, drop beneath the ship . . . rise against her bottom, attach the torpedo to it by screws, back off to a suitable distance . . . and fade away. The torpedo to work by clockwork, and when it strikes the hour . . . good night!"[4]

It is probable that the two preceding Mobile Bay reports referred to the *Hunley*. However, the possibility of there being a similar vessel operated by a different group of men cannot altogether be ruled out. In November 1863 a Confederate mail was captured by the Federals. Included among the letters was a set of plans "from the principal contractor for building torpedo vessels, giving instructions for the building of some west of the Mississippi River and for Texas."[5] The plans quite clearly depict a submarine vessel similar to—but definitely not—the *Hunley*. The origin and possible operations of this unknown predator of the seas are unknown.

Rear Admiral Dahlgren, commanding the South Atlantic Blockading Squadron, was well aware of the dangers posed by the Confederate surface and submersible torpedo boats. On December 3, 1863, Admiral Dahlgren issued the following order to all ironclads guarding Charleston harbor:

Picket Duty is to be performed by four monitors; two for each night. One of which is to be well advanced up the harbor, in a position suitable for preventing the entrance or departure of any vessel attempting to pass in or out of Charleston harbor; and for observing Sumter and Moultrie or movements in and about them; taking care at the same time not to get aground, and also to change the position when the weather appears to render it unsafe. The second monitor is to keep within proper supporting distance of the first, so as to render aid if needed.

Two tugs will be on duty each night to patrol the water in the vicinity of the monitors, going as far from them toward the Rebel positions as may be safe; their movements will be regulated by the picket commanders of the monitors.

As many armed boats as can be conveniently furnished by the wooden vessels present will report every evening before sunset at the flagship. At least two of them are to be armed with howitzers, the remainder with rifles, revolvers, bowie knives, etc. The boats should have muffled oars, and be prepared to stop shot holes, etc. One half of these will take post with the monitors on picket, the other half will remain for relief on board of vessels ... anchored conveniently for the purpose; where fire and suitable quarters for sleeping will be provided. Hot coffee is also to be served to boat's crews going to and returning from guard.

The boats on picket will be relieved at regular intervals through the night. Extreme vigilance is to be used when the water is smooth, but when there is much sea or the weather is very inclement, the discretion of the commanders of the picket monitors is to be used as to the time which the boats shall row guard; and when alongside the monitors the boat's crews may be permitted to take shelter on deck from the weather. ...

The general object of the monitors, tugs, and boats on picket is to enforce the blockade rigorously, and to watch and check the movements of the enemy by water, whenever it can be done; particularly to detect and destroy the torpedo boats, and the picket boats of the Rebels.[6]

On January 7, 1864, after receiving reliable reports from Confederate deserters that the Confederate submarine was then stalking the waters of Charleston harbor and ready for action, Admiral Dahlgren appended his previous order with the following:

> I have reliable information that the Rebels have two torpedo boats ready for service, which may be expected on the first night when the water is suitable for their movement. One of these is the *David* which attacked the *Ironsides* in October, the other is similar to it.
>
> There is also one of another kind, which is nearly submerged, and can be entirely so; it is intended to go under the bottoms of vessels and there operate.
>
> This is believed by my informant to be sure of well working, though from bad management it has hitherto met with accidents, and was lying off Mount Pleasant two nights since.
>
> There being every reason to expect a visit from some or all of these torpedoes, the greatest vigilance will be needed to guard against them.
>
> The ironclads must have their fenders rigged out, and their own boats in motion about them. A netting must also be dropped overboard from the ends of the fenders, kept down with shot, and extending along the whole length of the sides; howitzers loaded with canister on the decks and a calcium (light) for each monitor.
>
> The tugs and picket boats must be incessantly upon the lookout, when the water is not rough, whether the weather is clear or rainy.
>
> I observe the ironclads are not anchored so as to be entirely clear of each other's fire if opened suddenly in the dark. This must be corrected, and Captain Rowan will assign the monitors suitable positions for this purpose, particularly with reference to his own vessel.
>
> It is also advisable not to anchor in the deepest part of the channel; for by not leaving much space between the bottom of the vessel and the bottom of the channel, it will be impossible for the diving Torpedo to operate except on the sides, and there will be less difficulty in raising a vessel if sunk.[7]

The inner blockade consisting of ironclads was thus very well protected from Confederate torpedo craft. But what about the wooden gunboats of the outer blockade? In a letter to Captain Joseph Green of the *Canandaigua*, dated January 15, Admiral Dahlgren stated, "I can hardly think that the design would extend beyond the ironclads that constitute the inner blockade, for the outer vessels are distant and difficult of access. Still, it would be unwise to omit any proper precautions and I therefore advise that you will take such measures as may suffice to defeat any attempt of the kind."[8]

Appropriate measures were indeed taken. Despite the fact that the outer blockade did not incorporate picket boats, nor did the vessels utilize weighted rope nettings or similar contrivances cast over the sides as a means of prevention, the vessels were duly prepared for a possible torpedo attack.

On board the *Housatonic*, Captain Charles W. Pickering made sure his crew complied with Admiral Dahlgren's instructions and that his vessel was ready for action at a moment's notice. According to Executive Officer F. J. Higginson, "The general orders to the officer of the deck, passed through me, were that in case of discovering anything suspicious he was to slip the chain, beat to quarters, and back the engine as quickly as possible, at the same time informing the captain."

Like all other vessels of the blockading fleet, the *Housatonic* had previously been instructed by Admiral Dahlgren to maintain heavily banked fires through the night. The *Housatonic*'s engineers were required by Dahlgren's order to maintain 25 pounds of steam at all times, so the vessel could get under way at a moment's notice. On a previous occasion Captain Pickering had fouled his propeller on the slip rope by going forward. For this reason he issued the standing order to keep the engine reversed, ready for backing, while the ship lay at anchor at night.

On the night of February 17, as usual, six lookouts were posted on deck: one on each cathead, gangway, and quarter. Each lookout was armed with a rifle. In addition to the lookouts, the officer of the deck stood on the bridge, an officer was on the forecastle, and the quartermaster was on the quarterdeck; each was supplied with "night glasses." A quarter gunner was stationed to beat the gong for quarters and fire rockets. The remainder of the watch was on deck and armed as at quarters. Additionally, Captain Pickering related:

The Federal steam sloop-of-war Housatonic, *shown here in a drawing by R. G. Skerrett, was destroyed by the Confederate submarine* Hunley *on the night of February 17, 1864. The* Housatonic *sank within minutes of being torpedoed, but most of the officers and crew escaped by climbing the rigging, which projected above the shallow water.*

Two men were stationed at the slip rope, and others at the chain stopper and shackle on the spar deck. The chain was prepared for slipping by reversing the shackle, bow aft instead of forward. The pin which confined the bolt removed and a wooden pin substituted, and the shackle placed upon chain shoes, fair for knocking the bolt out; so that all that was necessary to slip the chain was to strike the bolt with the sledge once, which broke the wooden pin, and drove the bolt across the deck, leaving the forward end of the chain clear of the shackle.

The *Housatonic*'s guns were ready for use at a moment's notice. According to Captain Pickering, the "battery all cast loose and loaded; two shell, two canister and two grape were kept by each gun." Officer of the Deck John K. Crosby stated: "The 30 pounder Parrott gun on the forecastle was pivoted to port; the 100 pounder Parrott gun abaft the foremast was pivoted to starboard; the 11-inch gun between the main and mizzenmast was pivoted to port; the balance of the guns were broadside guns, and were cast loose with tackles hooked in the fighting bolts."

The steam sloop-of-war *Housatonic* was indeed ready at all points for immediate action. Against this most formidable enemy went the tiny *Hunley.* But was it really the *Hunley?* It would be well to establish beyond any reasonable doubt that it was, in fact, the *Hunley* and not the *David* or some similar craft which attacked the *Housatonic* on that night.

Acting Master's Mate Lewis Cornthwait, officer of the forecastle, had this to report about the object that attacked the *Housatonic:* "I then made it out with my glasses and it looked to me like a log with two bumps . . . on it, about 10 feet apart. There was a break of the water forward, aft, and between these two bumps."

To Executive Officer Higginson "it had the appearance of a plank sharp at both ends: it was entirely on a wash with the water, and there was a glimmer of light through the top of it, as though through a deadlight." Coxswain Henry S. Gifford, captain of the forecastle, saw something "about 25 or 30 feet long, sharp at both ends, with two protuberances about the size of mess kettles, each 10 feet from the end." And, to Robert F. Flemming, lookout on the starboard cathead, the object "appeared to be about 22 feet long, only each end visible, the water washing over amidships, each end about 22 inches out of water."

Considering the urgency and confusion on board the *Housatonic* during the sighting, it is not surprising that the eyewitness accounts vary somewhat in the object's description. Size estimates will naturally vary, as this is always a subjective judgment on the part of the observers. Estimates regarding the *Hunley*'s length, however, are further compli-cated by the fact that some individuals saw the entire hull of the vessel, while others assumed the vessel's length to be merely between the two "bumps."

These references to two "bumps" or "protuberances" being visible above the water establish with relative certainty that the unknown attacker was the CSS *Hunley.* Only this craft possessed two hatches that would be visible on the water's surface while operating in an awash position. As was explained in the description in the preceding chapter, the *Hunley* would naturally appear "sharp at both ends, with a break of water forward, aft, and amidships."

Note that while the executive officer, Lieutenant Higginson, did not mention the projections per se, he did mention seeing a "glimmer of light through the top of it, as though *through* a deadlight." And a deadlight it was! Recall that while the *Hunley* was in operation, a candle burned near the commander, illuminating the controls and indicating the amount of remaining oxygen. Surely it was light given off by this candle which Lieutenant Higginson observed, not through an open hatch cover, as has been implied by other writers, but through one of the thick pieces of glass set in the hatch combing for observation: a "deadlight."

The last piece of evidence to consider is not what was seen, but rather what was *not heard.* The *David*s were steam powered. The noise generated by the steam engine would most certainly have been audible to the *Housatonic's* crew. And yet, not a single individual mentioned hearing a noise of *any kind* emitted by the torpedo boat. The manually propelled *Hunley* would have slipped noiselessly through the water.

All these facts serve to identify the vessel as the *Hunley.* The eyewitness descriptions simply do not come close to matching the *David* or any other Confederate vessel known to be operating in Charleston harbor at that time. The descriptions do, however, match the *Hunley*'s appearance as related by William Alexander, James McClintock, and Colonel Olmstead. It therefore seems conclusive that it was indeed the CSS *Hunley* that struck out that night to seek mischief among the Federal blockading fleet.

What transpired on board the *Housatonic* as the *Hunley* drew near? Acting Master John K. Crosby was officer of the deck; his testimony has gone down in the pages of history:

About 8:45 P.M. I saw something on the water, which at first looked to me like a porpoise, coming up to the surface to blow. It was about 75 to 100 yards from us on our starboard beam, the ship heading northwest by west 1/2 west at the time, the wind 2 or 3 points on the starboard bow. At that moment I called the quartermaster's attention to it asking him if he saw anything. He looked at it through his glass and said he saw nothing but a tide ripple on the water. Looking again within an instant, I saw it was coming towards the ship very fast. I gave orders to beat to quarters, slip the chain, and back the engine; the orders being executed immediately.

At this time the officer of the forecastle, Acting Master's Mate L. A. Cornthwait, came aft and reported seeing this object on the water. At the same time I informed the captain that I saw something on the water coming towards the ship very fast, but could not make out what it was. About this time the executive officer, Lieutenant Higginson, came up on the bridge and asked me what I had seen. I told him I saw a swash on the water, but could not tell what it was. Captain Pickering then came on deck, gave orders to slip the chain and back the engine, and asked me what I had seen. I told him I saw something in the water that looked like a tide ripple or a porpoise, but I could not tell what it was.

I then jumped down off the bridge, the executive officer having taken the deck, and started to go forward to see that the chain had been slipped. As I was going forward I looked over the side. I saw what appeared to me a plank sharp at both ends, about 20 feet from the ship's side. I went forward, and, as I was coming aft again, the explosion took place. After I gave the order to go to quarters several muskets were fired at it, and when it was close alongside Captain Pickering fired his gun at it. I don't think it was over 2 1/2 or 3 minutes from the time I first saw the object on the water until it struck, just abaft the mizzenmast, on the starboard side and the explosion took place.

Crosby's testimony, while no doubt a factual account of what he observed and the actions he took, cannot tell the entire story of what happened on that night. To fully appreciate the events leading up to the *Hunley*'s attack it is necessary to examine the testimonies of others on board the *Housatonic* at the time of the attack.

According to his account, Crosby independently discovered an object fast approaching the huge warship. But prior to Crosby's sighting, and completely unknown to him, a drama was unfolding on the starboard bow of the *Housatonic.* The characters included Robert F. Flemming, Lewis A. Cornthwait, and the CSS *Hunley.*

At approximately 8:25 P.M., the sharp eyes of Robert Flemming, stationed as lookout on the starboard cathead, detected something approaching the ship off the starboard bow, about two ship's lengths off. He promptly reported his sighting to Lewis Cornthwait, officer of the forecastle. But Cornthwait thought the object Flemming had sighted was merely a log. Although Flemming then informed him that the object "was not floating with the tide as a log would, but moving across the tide," Cornthwait still thought it was a log.

Frustrated with Cornthwait's lack of concern, Flemming called the lookout from the port cathead to see what the strange object was. C. P. Slade was that lookout, and according to his testimony: "The lookout on the starboard cathead called me over and said there was a torpedo coming. I went over and looked at it; it was about 1 1/2 ship's lengths off the starboard beam, moving rather fast, towards the after pivot gun's port . . . the master's mate [Cornthwait] was on the top-gallant forecastle at the time, talking to the captain of the forecastle [Gifford]."

Cooper George Kelly was not on watch at the time of Flemming's sighting, but happened to be on deck. "Before I went on the forecastle," Kelly testified, "I heard the lookout on the starboard cathead say he saw a droll-looking log *moving across the tide.* Afterwards I heard him say, '*If no one is going to report this, I will cut the buoy adrift myself and get ready for slipping.*' These remarks were what attracted my attention" (italics added).

Seaman Thomas Kelly, stationed with a slow match to fire rockets in an emergency and to beat the gong for quarters, also overheard the dialogue between Flemming and Cornthwait. "About 8:45 P.M., I was by the after pivot gun," reported Kelly, "*when I heard the lookout on the starboard cathead report seeing something like a log coming towards the ship. Mr. Cornthwait replied it was nothing but a log*" (italics added). Kelly's testimony in the *Proceedings of the Naval Court of Inquiry* continues:

QUESTION BY THE COURT: When you heard the lookout at the cathead report the object in the water, to whom did he report it, and what were the words of his report?

ANSWER: To Mr. Cornthwait, officer of the forecastle. He said, "There is something coming that looks like a log: it looks very suspicious."

QUESTION BY THE COURT: Where was Mr. Cornthwait at the time the report was made to him, and was the report made to him in a moderate or loud tone of voice?

ANSWER: He was on the forecastle. The report was made in a loud tone.

QUESTION BY THE COURT: How near to the after pivot gun were you when you heard the report made to Mr. Cornthwait?

ANSWER: About 15 feet forward of it: I was abaft the mainmast.

QUESTION BY THE COURT: You have stated you were near the after pivot gun at the time this report was made to Mr. Cornthwait. How then do you know that the lookout at the cathead made this report, and that it was made to Mr. Cornthwait?

ANSWER: I heard the lookout call Mr. Cornthwait's name, and I saw him on the forecastle.

As might be anticipated, Lewis Cornthwait's testimony differs significantly from those previously cited and from others to follow. According to Cornthwait:

I went on watch on the forecastle at 8 P.M. . . . . about 8:45 the lookout on the starboard cathead reported something adrift on the water, about 2 points on the starboard bow, and about 100 yards distant. . . .

As soon as I saw it, I ran aft and reported it to the officer of the deck, who was on the bridge, and his glass turned in the direction of this object. I asked him if he saw it, and he replied 'Call all hands to quarters.' I then called the quarter gunner, and told him to beat the gong.

The order was then given to slip the chain. I ran forward, knocked the pin out of the shackle, and reported the chain slipped, though at that time it had not run out. Immediately, the inquiry was made from the quarter-deck whether the chain was slipped: it began to run out of the hawse pipe and I ran aft to report it. When I got abreast the engine-room hatch the explosion took place. There was a general rush forward, and I ran with the crowd.

In a detailed study of the *Proceedings of the Naval Court of Inquiry*, the discrepancies with Lewis Cornthwait's account become apparent. First, Cornthwait claimed to have reported the strange object "*as soon as he saw it.*" Second, he claimed to have reported the object to the officer of the deck (John Crosby) *before the order was given to call* all hands to quarters. And third, Cornthwait claimed it was he who "*called the quarter gunner, and told him to beat the gong*" for quarters (italics added). In light of other evidence, these claims bear little weight.

The testimonies of Robert Flemming, George Kelly, and Thomas Kelly clearly demonstrate that Flemming initially discovered a strange object approaching the ship and promptly reported the sighting to Lewis Cornthwait. Convinced the object was nothing but a log, Cornthwait did not actually "run aft as soon as he saw it." Instead, and contrary to orders, Cornthwait initially took no action at all.

It will be recalled that Flemming, frustrated with Cornthwait's unconcern, called the lookout on the port cathead over to see the suspicious object. "When the officer of the forecastle saw this other lookout coming over, he looked at the object through his glasses and then ran aft," reported Flemming. "I then cut away the slip buoy. By this time the object had got within about 30 feet of the starboard quarter. They beat to quarters."

Flemming estimated one and one-half minutes elapsed from his initial sighting until Cornthwait finally headed aft to make a report. Other eyewitnesses estimated a longer delay. The lookout on the port cathead, C. P. Slade, claimed: "Three minutes after I went over to the starboard side, he [Lewis Cornthwait] went aft and soon after they beat to quarters."

Quarter Gunner Thomas Kelly estimated *ten* minutes passed between the time he heard the lookout's report until he was given the order to call the crew to quarters. In all likelihood, ten minutes is an innocent exaggeration. The important point here, however, is that a period of time, perhaps several minutes in duration, did elapse from Flemming's sighting until further action was taken. Furthermore, the action that was then taken was not due to Flemming's observation, but was due to Crosby's independent discovery. In short, news of Flemming's sighting—via Lewis Cornthwait—did not reach Crosby until it was too late. The minutes that were lost might have allowed the *Housatonic*'s crew to ward off the *Hunley*'s attack, maybe even to destroy the submarine.

"If the object had been reported when it was first discovered," suggested Thomas Kelly, "the number four gun—100 pounder pivot gun between the fore and main rigging—might have been trained on it."

And Captain Pickering claimed, "If I had had two minutes to work in, I could probably have saved the ship and sunk the Torpedo craft."

If Cornthwait had not hesitated, Pickering would have had the time he so desperately needed. But the time remaining after Crosby independently sighted the submarine was too little to do much of anything.

As to Cornthwait's claims that he reported the object to the officer of the deck (John Crosby) before the order was given to call all hands to quarters, and that he was the one to give that order, the two can be treated together. In his earlier testimony, Crosby clearly states it was he, not Cornthwait, who gave the order. Crosby further indicates that Cornthwait, in fact, arrived after the order was given.

"I gave orders to beat to quarters, slip the chain, and back the engine," reported Crosby, "the orders being executed immediately. At this time the officer of the forecastle, Acting Master's Mate Lewis Cornthwait, came aft and reported seeing this object on the water."

Henry Gifford, who was on the forecastle talking with Cornthwait when Flemming's initial sighting was made, also states it was Crosby, not Cornthwait, who gave the order: "Just then I heard *Mr. Crosby* give orders to beat the gong, slip the chain, and ring three bells [to back the engine]." Further, Flemming states that Cornthwait "left the forecastle, *but did not get aft before they beat to quarters*" (italics added).

The final, conclusive evidence comes from the testimony of Thomas

Kelly, the quarter gunner who received and carried out the order. "About 10 minutes afterwards, I heard Mr. Crosby ask the quartermaster what was that coming. I then went directly to the starboard port of the after pivot gun, looked over the side, and saw an object in the water. . . . I sang out 'That's a torpedo,' and *Mr. Crosby told me to beat to quarters, and gave orders to slip the chain*" (italics added).

Thus, it appears that sometime prior to 8:45 P.M., Robert Flemming made the initial sighting of the *Hunley*. Flemming promptly reported his observation to Lewis Cornthwait, who believed the object was merely a log and neglected to act upon the report. At approximately 8:45, John Crosby independently discovered the object. Within seconds of his discovery, Crosby issued orders to beat the gong for quarters, slip the chain, and back the engine, and he sent a messenger to inform Captain Pickering. Shortly after Crosby gave these orders, Lewis Cornthwait arrived and reported seeing the object.

Moments later, Executive Officer Higginson arrived on deck, followed shortly thereafter by Captain Pickering. After explaining what he had observed, Crosby relinquished his command and went forward to see if the chain had been slipped. According to Lieutenant Higginson: "I went on deck immediately, found the officer of the deck on the bridge, and asked him the cause of the alarm. He pointed abaft the starboard beam on the water and said there it is. . . . About a minute after the officer of the deck gave the order the cable was slipped, and the propeller was in motion about the same time."

While the propeller was in motion shortly after the orders were given, there was little time to move the vessel before the *Hunley*'s torpedo exploded. Third Assistant Engineer James W. Holihan related:

I took charge of the watch in the engine room at 8 P.M. . . . The orders were fully carried out on that night: to the best of my knowledge there was a little over 25 pounds of steam on, as we endeavored always to be rather over than under the mark. The fires were heavily banked and in good order. . . . I was [in the engine room]. I heard the gong beat for quarters, and gave orders to have everything ready for starting the engine. Immediately three bells were struck, and I gave orders to open the stop valves and back the engine. The engine had made about 10 revolutions, at the rate of about 30 per minute, before the explosion took place.

Had the explosion not occurred, claimed Holihan, "we could have made about 52 revolutions per minute, which would have driven her about 7 1/2 knots at the start, and we could have increased it gradually to 8 1/2 knots." If the orders to slip the chain and back the engine had been given when the *Hunley* was first sighted by Robert Flemming, the *Housatonic* could have gained sufficient speed to escape its attacker. As it was, the *Housatonic*'s propeller barely had time to begin churning the water before the torpedo took its deadly toll.

Regarding the incident on board the *Housatonic*, Captain Charles W. Pickering had the following to report:

> While seated at the cabin table overhauling a book of charts, I heard a confused sound and stir of excitement on deck. I heard the officer of the deck call the orderly for the transmission of some information. I sprang from the table under the impression that a blockade runner was about. In snatching my cap I found I had taken Dr. Plant's by mistake, who was seated at the table with me at the time. I turned back, got my own, met the orderly at the cabin door, and passed him without waiting to receive his report.
>
> On reaching the deck I gave the order to slip, and heard for the first time it was a torpedo, I think from the officer of the deck. I repeated the order to go astern, and to open fire. I turned instantly, took my double barrelled gun loaded with buck shot, from Mr. Muzzey, my aid and clerk, and jumped up on the horseblock on the starboard quarter, which [Lieutenant Higginson] had just left, having fired a musket at the torpedo. . . .
>
> I fired at these [projections], jumped down from the horseblock, and ran up the port side of the quarter-deck, as far as the mizzenmast, singing out "Go astern faster."
>
> The men were huddling forward. I would not call them aft to the guns, as they could not be trained until the ship had got some distance from the torpedo, and they were in a safer place.

I thought of going forward myself to get clear of the torpedo, but, reflecting that my proper station was aft, I remained there, and was blown into the air the next instant from where I stood on the port side abreast of the mizzenmast.

Most eyewitness accounts agree that the explosion took place approximately three minutes after Crosby gave the order for quarters. The effects of the explosion on the *Housatonic* were spectacular. "The ship was shaken violently, and caused to sink immediately, settling by the stern, heeling over to port as she sank," reported Lieutenant Higginson. "Many articles about the deck floated off and drifted astern when she sank. I heard a report, not very loud, a low stunning crash, a smothered sound."

According to John Crosby, "The ship commenced filling as soon as the explosion took place. . . . The explosion started me off my feet, as if the ship had struck hard on the bottom. I saw fragments of the wreck going up into the air. I saw no column of water thrown up, no smoke, and no flame. There was no sharp report, but it sounded like a collision with another vessel."

While others reported seeing a heavy black smoke, no one saw any flame, nor did anyone see a column of water thrown up. Unlike the attempt against the *Ironsides* when the *David*'s torpedo literally bounced off the hull and exploded several feet away, the *Hunley*'s torpedo exploded directly against the *Housatonic*. The full destructive force was directed against its wooden hull, and the *Housatonic*'s side was instantly blown apart. Five minutes later the once-mighty ship was resting on the bottom off Charleston harbor. Fortunately, the water was not very deep, and all but five of the crew managed to save themselves by climbing into the rigging:

At 9:20 p.m. discovered a boat pulling toward us. Hailed her and found her to be from the *Housatonic*. She reported the *Housatonic* sunk by a torpedo. Immediately slipped our chain and started for the scene of danger, with the *Housatonic*'s boat in tow. At the same time sent up three rockets and burned Coston signals No. 82 and soon after burned 82 again.

At 9:30 P.M. picked up another boat from the *Housatonic*, with Captain Pickering on board. At 9:35 arrived at the *Housatonic* and found her sunk. Lowered all boats, sent them alongside, and rescued the officers and crew, clinging to the rigging. At 10:30 all were brought from the wreck.[9]

In the chaos after the explosion, 150 men scrambled to safety as the ship quickly settled on the bottom. Five men did not. Ensign Edward C. Hazeltine, Captain's Clerk Charles O. Muzzey, Quartermaster John Williams, Landsman Theodore Parker, and Second-Class Fireman John Walsh perished with their ship.

4

The Mysterious Disappearance
of the *H. L. Hunley*

The United States sloop of war was attacked and destroyed on the night of the 17th of February. Since that time no information has been received of either the [attacking] boat or crew. I am of the opinion that, the torpedoes being placed at the bow of the boat, she went into the hole made in the *Housatonic* by explosion of torpedoes and did not have sufficient power to back out, consequently sunk with her.

—Captain M. M. Gray

One hundred twenty-six years ago, the *Hunley* slid beneath the troubled waters off Charleston harbor for the last time. Amid torrents of seawater and the rush of escaping air, the submarine sank to the bottom, never to be seen again. Somewhere, somehow, the *Hunley* inexplicably vanished after attacking the Federal warship *Housatonic.*

William Alexander, intimately acquainted with the *Hunley*'s design and operation, offered the following explanation for its mysterious disappearance:

Next came the news that on February 17 the submarine torpedo boat *Hunley* had sunk the United States sloop-of-war *Housatonic* outside the bar off Charleston, S.C. . . . although it was moonlight, Dixon, who had been waiting so long for a change of wind, took the risk of the moonlight and went out. The lookout on the ship saw him when he came to the surface for his final observation before striking her. He, of course, not knowing that the ship had slipped her chain and was backing down upon him, then sank the boat a few feet, steered for the stern of the ship and struck. The momentum of the two vessels brought them together unexpectedly. The stern of the ship was blown off entirely. The momentum carried the torpedo boat into the wreck. Dixon and his men, unable to extricate themselves, sinking with it.[1]

The first theory to account for the *Hunley*'s disappearance actually appeared in a letter dated April 29, 1864, written by Captain M. M. Gray of the Submarine Defense Office in Charleston, South Carolina. Gray was in charge of torpedoes and was responding to an inquiry from Major General Dabney H. Maury in Mobile, Alabama, regarding the loss of the *Hunley.* "I am of the opinion," wrote Gray, "that the torpedoes being placed at the bow of the boat, she went into the hole made in the *Housatonic* by explosion of torpedoes and did not have sufficient power to back out, consequently sunk with her." Alexander apparently accepted Gray's theory and embellished it with additional thoughts of his own.

Captain Gray's theory gained further support in 1865 when First Assistant Engineer James H. Tomb recorded the following:

> There was a submarine torpedo boat, not under the orders of the Navy, and I was ordered to tow her down the harbor three or four times by Flag-Officer Tucker, who also gave me orders to report as to her efficiency as well as safety. In my report to him I stated, "the only way to use a torpedo was on the same plan as the *David*—that is, a spar torpedo—and to strike with his boat on the surface, the torpedo being lowered to 8 feet. Should she attempt to use a torpedo as Lieutenant Dixon intended, by submerging the boat and striking from below, the level of the torpedo would be above his own boat, and as she had little buoyancy and no power, the chances were the suction caused by the water passing into the sinking

ship would prevent her rising to the surface, besides the possibility of his own boat being disabled.[2]

While at first glance Captain Gray's explanation of the *Hunley*'s disappearance seems plausible—and it has generally been accepted as fact—further study shows this is not what really happened. These early theories concerning the *Hunley*'s fate were based solely upon supposition, not evidence. Using all currently available evidence, it is possible to prove that the *Hunley* did not sink alongside its victim. As an important part of that proof, evidence will be examined showing that the *Hunley*'s torpedo did not explode at the moment of impact, but that the *Hunley* had actually backed a safe distance from the doomed *Housatonic* prior to the detonation. In all likelihood, the submarine was actually returning to port when some unfortunate accident sent it quickly and unceremoniously to the muddy bottom off Charleston harbor.

The generally accepted conclusion that the *Housatonic* abruptly backed into the unsuspecting *Hunley* is in error. Alexander claimed that Lieutenant Dixon, "not knowing that the ship had slipped her chain *and was backing down upon him,* then sank the boat a few feet, steered for the stern and struck. The momentum of the two vessels *brought them together unexpectedly. . . .* The momentum *carried the torpedo boat into the wreck"* (italics added). However, according to eyewitness accounts, this could not have happened.

First, according to Third Assistant Engineer James W. Holihan, the *Housatonic*'s engine was only in motion for about ten seconds before the explosion occurred.[3] In those few seconds the propeller had gone from a dead stop to a rate of only thirty revolutions per minute. The *Housatonic* certainly could not have picked up much speed nor traveled very far in such a brief time.

Second, according to eyewitness accounts, the *Hunley* approached the *Housatonic* from the starboard side *at right angles to the ship's keel.* Even if the great warship had picked up sufficient sternway, this motion would not have brought the two vessels together. Instead, the *Housatonic* would have slipped past the *Hunley* at a right angle. The momentum (what little there was) did not unexpectedly bring the two vessels together nor "carry the torpedo-boat into the wreck."

Third, the *Hunley*'s torpedo did not explode on impact with the little submarine in close proximity to the hull of the *Housatonic.* The evidence strongly indicates that the *Hunley* approached the *Housatonic,* affixed the torpedo to its victim's hull, and then backed away prior to the explosion. According to a report written by Executive Officer Higginson on February 18, 1864, the day after the sinking, the *Hunley*'s torpedo did not explode for nearly a minute after the submarine approached the *Housatonic*:

> About 8:45 P.M., the officer of the deck, Acting Master J. K. Crosby, discovered something in the water about 100 yards from and moving toward the ship. It had the appearance of a plank moving in the water. It came directly toward the ship, *the time from when it was first seen till it was close alongside* being about 2 minutes.
>
> During this time the chain was slipped, engine backed, and all hands called to quarters. The torpedo struck the ship forward of the mizzenmast, on the starboard side, in a line with the magazine.
>
> *About one minute after she was close alongside the explosion took place*, the ship sinking stern first and heeling to port as she sank (italics added).[4]

Regarding the *Hunley*'s movements at the time of the explosion, Lieutenant Higginson sheds a little more light on the subject in his testimony before the Naval Court of Inquiry. "I then saw something resembling a plank, moving towards the ship at the rate of 3 or 4 knots," reported Higginson. "*It came close alongside, a little forward of the mizzenmast on the starboard side. It then stopped, and appeared to move off slowly*" (italics added).

In his testimony before the court, Captain Charles Pickering further supports the premise that the *Hunley*'s torpedo did not explode on impact but rather at a later time. "Its position was at right angles to the ship, bows on, and the bows within 3 or 4 feet of the ship's side, about abreast of the mizzenmast, *and I supposed it was then fixing the torpedo on"* (italics added).

Ensign Charles Craven provides the most conclusive proof that the *Hunley* came alongside the *Housatonic,* then backed away before the explosion occurred. Craven fired his revolver at the submarine while it was close alongside, and then attempted to fire the number six gun at the submarine after it had backed away. According to Craven's testimony in the *Proceedings of the Naval Court of Inquiry:*

> I was in my room about 9 p.m. . . . when I heard the officer of the deck give the order "Call all hands to quarters." I went on deck and saw something in the water on the starboard side of the ship, making towards the ship, about 30 feet off, and the captain and executive officer were firing at it. It looked to me like a water logged plank. . . .
>
> *I fired two shots at her with my revolver as she was standing towards the ship as soon as I saw her, and a third shot when she was almost under the counter, having to lean over the port to fire it.* I then went to my division, which is the second, and consists of four broadside 32 pounder guns in the waist, and tried with the captain of number 6 gun to train it on this object, *as she was backing from the ship, and about 40 or 50 feet off then.* I had nearly succeeded, and was about to pull the lock string when the explosion took place (italics added).

If, indeed, the *Hunley* approached the *Housatonic* and then backed away prior to the explosion as the evidence indicates, the question arises as to what type of torpedo was used for the attack. Modern historians have claimed all kinds of torpedoes as the *Hunley*'s armament, from electric torpedoes to clever devices screwed to the *Housatonic*'s hull and detonated by time delay fuses. At least one writer has claimed that the *Hunley*'s mode of attack involved "towing a floating torpedo to be *exploded by means of electricity* as soon as it touched the keel," but this was undoubtedly not the case.

The electric torpedo typically consisted of a very large watertight cylinder containing up to two thousand pounds of powder. Placed in operation by courageous members of the Confederate Torpedo Corps, the torpedo would be submerged about 10 feet below the water's surface. Wires ran to a powerful voltaic battery hidden on the shore, which ignited the explosive. At the mere closing of a switch the torpedo would detonate, and any unfortunate vessel located on the water above would be blown to bits.

Although the electric torpedo met with fair success defending many of the South's inland waterways, including the spectacular destruction of the Federal ironclad *Cairo* in the Yazoo River during December 1862, this device proved impossible armament for the tiny *Hunley.* While the electric charge could have been applied to torpedoes small enough to be handled by the submarine (torpedoes with around 90 pounds of explosives), the voltaic batteries at that time were extremely large, bulky, and heavy. Even the smallest battery, with just enough power to ignite the powder, could not have been taken on board the *Hunley* due to size and weight constraints.

While a floating *electric* torpedo was definitely out of the question, a floating *contact* torpedo was not. General Beauregard, intimately associated with the submarine while it operated in Charleston harbor, described the early method of torpedo delivery: "As originally designed, the torpedo was to be dragged astern upon the surface of the water; the boat, approaching the broadside of the vessel to be attacked, was to dive beneath it, and, rising to the surface beyond, continue its course, thus bringing the floating torpedo against the vessel's side, when it would be discharged by a trigger contrived to go off by the contact."[5]

The *Hunley*'s early use of a floating torpedo is further substantiated by William Alexander, who also described a second mode of torpedo delivery:

> The torpedo was a copper cylinder holding a charge of 90 pounds of explosive, with percussion and friction primer mechanism, set off by flaring triggers. It was originally intended to float the torpedo on the surface of the water, the boat to dive under the vessel to be attacked, towing the torpedo with a line 200 feet after her, one of the triggers to touch the vessel and explode the torpedo, and in the experiments made in the smooth water of Mobile River on some old flatboats these plans operated success-

fully, but in rough water the torpedo was continually coming too near the wrong boat. We then rigged a yellow-pine boom, 22 feet long and tapering. This was attached to the bow, banded and guyed on each side. A socket on the torpedo secured it to the boom.[6]

The South was instrumental in developing torpedoes and applying them to wartime use, both offensively and defensively. Submarine mines, then referred to as torpedoes, were little known in the military world. At the start of the war, the South, severely lacking an established navy, sorely needed a means of defending her rivers and harbors against invasion by the enemy.

Through the efforts of Stephen R. Mallory, Secretary of the fledgling Confederate States Navy, torpedo warfare gained the support of the Confederate government. Captain Matthew Fontaine Maury was placed in charge of the early experiments, and the Torpedo Corps was formed. Finally, in October 1862, the Torpedo Bureau was officially established. General Gabriel J. Rains was placed in charge, and wartime production of the new, potentially lethal devices was begun.

And lethal they proved to be. A torpedo utilizes a concussive force to effectively collapse the hull of its victim. Upon detonation, the tremendous pressure developed by the released gases follows the path offering the least resistance. The gases rush to the water's surface, where their terrible energy is released in the form of a water geyser. If the explosion occurs far enough below the water's surface and next to a vessel's hull, before the gases can reach the surface their explosive energy will be directed against the hull. As the surrounding water can be compressed only slightly, the tremendous pressure released will cave in the victim's hull.

The contact fuses for these early torpedoes were typically about 3 inches long and 1 inch in diameter. The tubes were constructed of sheet-lead and open at one end—the end that was embedded in the powder. The other end was sealed with a rounded piece of lead, of much thinner construction than the walls of the tube. A small glass vial filled with sulphuric acid was fitted into the tube and hermetically sealed. The space between the glass vial and lead tube was tightly packed with a mixture of potash and pulverized white sugar.

Each fuse was carefully inserted into a hole in the torpedo, embedded in the gunpowder, and sealed in place. When the round end of the fuse struck a hard object, the thin lead would readily dent and break the glass vial located within. As the sulphuric acid came into contact with the mixture of potash and sugar, a violent reaction would occur and ignite the gunpowder.[7]

According to General Beauregard, after the tragic accident that claimed Captain Hunley and his crew, the floating torpedo was replaced with a spar torpedo invented by Captain Francis D. Lee. Alexander's description of the torpedo as a "copper cylinder holding a charge of 90 pounds of explosive, with percussion and friction primer mechanism, set off by flaring triggers" certainly matches that of a Lee spar torpedo. But was a Lee torpedo actually used for the attack upon the *Housatonic?*

The Lee spar torpedo, placed on many Confederate vessels, was designed to explode on impact, the flaring triggers detonating the packed explosive. The victim would be approached at slow speed to allow the attacking vessel to reverse direction immediately upon the torpedo's detonation. However, according to eyewitness accounts on board the *Housatonic,* the *Hunley* approached the ship, then backed off *before the explosion occurred.* The torpedo did not explode on contact. Therefore, the torpedo used to destroy the *Housatonic* was either one designed by someone else or a modified Lee spar torpedo.

The first piece of evidence supporting this claim comes from a letter written by J. D. Breaman to his wife on March 3, 1864.[8] Breaman, part owner of the *Hunley,* was a member of the special engineer corps engaged in "the special service of destroying the enemy's property by torpedoes and similar inventions."[9]

> Since we have been on this side of the river, we have gotten up a great many projects and have been interested in many new schemes, the particulars of which are too lengthy for an ordinary letter. Among the number, however, was a submarine boat, built at this place, of which Whitney and myself bought one-fifth for $3000. . . .

A few nights ago he [Lieutenant Dixon] went out, attacked and sunk the steam sloop-of-war *Housatonic*, but . . . fear that he and his crew were all lost. I enclose a slip from our paper, giving an account of the affair, which will be interesting to you, *as Singer and myself built the torpedoes with which the ship was destroyed*, and besides, we own a considerable interest in the value of the ship, as the owners and crew of the boat got one-half of her value for destroying her (italics added).

The second scrap of evidence suggesting a standard spar torpedo was not used for the *Housatonic* attack appears in a letter dated January 13, 1864, written by Admiral Dahlgren.[10] Dahlgren had received several fairly accurate reports concerning the *Hunley* from Confederate deserters, and wrote, "It [the *Hunley*] is intended to submerge completely, get under the bottom, *attach the torpedo, haul off and pull trigger*" (italics added).

The last, and most conclusive, piece of evidence is from a letter dated at Mobile, August 24, 1863. General Dabney H. Maury, commander of the Department of the Gulf, wrote to General Joseph E. Johnston: "The submarine boat sent to Charleston found that there was not water enough under the *Ironsides* for her to pass below the keel; therefore, they decided to affix a spike to the bow of the boat, to drive the spike into the *Ironsides, then to back out, and by a string to explode the torpedo which was to be attached to the spike*" (italics added).[11]

Lieutenant Dixon was no doubt aware of the dangers involved with exploding a spar torpedo on impact. In addition to the dangerous suction created by the sinking ship, the concussion of the blast could wreak havoc with the little submarine if in close proximity. The use of a "spike" or "spear-headed" torpedo—in which the detonation would occur only after the submarine had backed a safe distance away—would eliminate these dangers. Such a spear-headed torpedo was described by Harry von Kolnitz in his *U.S. Naval Institute Proceedings* article of October 1937:

It consisted of a steel head which fitted as a thimble over the end of the 10-foot spar or pipe projecting from the bow. This was driven into the enemy's wooden hull by ramming and was retained there by saw-toothed corrugations when the fish boat backed off. As it slipped off the spar, it would keep with it the torpedo, which was a simple copper can of powder fitted with a trigger. This trigger was attached to a cord lanyard carried on a reel on deck and after the boat had backed a safe distance, 150 yards, the rope was to tighten and would trip the trigger.

It appears that Lieutenant Dixon incorporated just such a torpedo for the attack upon the *Housatonic*. Based upon the eyewitness reports cited earlier, Lieutenant Dixon apparently approached the *Housatonic*, drove the spike with attached torpedo deep into the vessel's wooden hull, then backed off to a safe distance before detonating the torpedo by means of a lanyard. If this were indeed the case, it may be assumed that the *Hunley* was not sucked into the gaping hole created by the blast, and therefore did not sink alongside the *Housatonic*. There is ample evidence supporting this assumption.

The submarine was not found lodged in the hole created in the *Housatonic*, as some writers have claimed. Indeed, the wreck of the *H. L. Hunley* has never been located. The earliest examination of the wreck of the *Housatonic* was made by Captain Joseph F. Green on February 20, 1864, just three days after she sank. In his report, Green made no mention of the submarine:

> I have examined the wreck of the *Housatonic* this morning and find her spar deck about 15 feet below the surface of the water. The after part of her spar deck appears to have been entirely blown off.
>
> Her guns, etc., on the spar deck, can, in my opinion, be recovered by the employment for the purpose of the derrick boat and divers.[12]

A much more detailed examination of the wreck was made in November 1864, by Lieutenant W. L. Churchill. Although Churchill deliberately searched for the submarine, not a trace of it was found:

> The *Housatonic* is very much worm-eaten, as I find from pieces which

have been brought up. She is in an upright position; has settled in the sand about 5 feet, forming a bank of mud and sand around her bed; the mud has collected in her in small quantities. The cabin is completely demolished, as are also all the bulkheads abaft the mainmast; the coal is scattered about her lower decks in heaps, as well as muskets, small arms, and quantities of rubbish.

I tried to find the magazine, but the weather has been so unfavorable and the swell so great that it was not safe to keep a diver in the wreck. I took advantage of all the good weather that I had, and examined as much as was possible.

The propeller is in an upright position; the shaft appears to be broken. The rudderpost and rudder have been partly blown off; the upper parts of both are in their proper places, while the lower parts have been forced aft. The stern frame rests upon the rudderpost and propeller; any part of it can be easily slung with chain slings, and a powerful steamer can detach each part.

I have also caused the bottom to be dragged for an area of 500 yards around the wreck, finding nothing of the torpedo boat. On the 24th the drag ropes caught something heavy (as I reported). On sending a diver down to examine it, proved to be a quantity of rubbish. The examination being completed, I could accomplish nothing further, unless it is the intention to raise the wreck or propeller, in which case it will be necessary to have more machinery (italics added).[13]

Eight years later, when the ship-channel at Charleston was being improved, the U.S. Army Corps of Engineers released a contract for "the removal of the wreck of the wooden gunboat *Housatonic* and the wreck of a torpedo boat near by." While the wreck of the *Housatonic* was removed, "the torpedo boat . . . could not be found."[14]

To be more accurate, the wreck of the *Housatonic* was actually cut down and removed to a depth of 20 feet below mean low water in 1872. The lower portion of the wreck remained, and occasionally interfered with the passage of ships in the channel. In 1909, the government decided to remove an additional seven feet of the wreck, and the necessary work was begun. William H. Virden blasted the boilers, "which was practically all that remained of the wreck, breaking them into pieces," and hauled them away.

Some historians have speculated that the *Hunley* was mistaken for the ship's boilers and consequently blown up. If this were true, it seems strange that the submarine would have gone unnoticed during examinations in both 1864 and 1872. Be that as it may, there is additional evidence indicating the *Hunley* did not sink alongside the *Housatonic*. Indeed, it appears that the *Hunley* not only survived the attack upon the *Housatonic*, but was actually returning to port when some unfortunate accident befell it.

In the confusion and panic immediately following the explosion onboard the stricken *Housatonic*, few men thought to look over the side at their attacker. One man who did, however, was Robert Flemming, the lookout on the starboard cathead who had initially sighted the submarine. "I ran aft and before I got to my quarters, at number 7 gun, the explosion took place," reported Flemming. "The ship began to settle by the stern immediately, and I ran forward again, and when I got on the forecastle *I saw the object* about 6 or 8 feet from the starboard quarter, apparently stationary, and I fired my gun at it" (italics added).

Flemming further stated: "When the [rescue ship] *Canandaigua* got astern, and lying athwart, of the *Housatonic*, about 4 shiplengths off, while I was in the rigging, I saw a blue light on the water just ahead of the *Canandaigua*, and on the starboard quarter of the *Housatonic*."

This statement by Robert Flemming may at first glance seem unimportant, until the following is noted: "The day of the night the perilous undertaking was accomplished, the little war vessel was taken to Breach Inlet. *The officer in command told Lieutenant-Colonel Dantzler when they bid each other good-by, that if he came off safe he would show two blue lights* (italics added)."[15] Lieutenant-Colonel O. M. Dantzler confirms the signal arrangement, and further states that the *Hunley*'s signals were observed after the attack, in a report written on February 19, 1864:

I have the honor to report that the torpedo boat stationed at this post went out on the night of the 17th instant (Wednesday) and has not yet returned. The signals agreed upon to be given in case the boat wished a light to be exposed at this post as a guide for its return *were observed and answered.* An earlier report would have been made of this matter, but the officer of the day for yesterday *was under the impression that the boat had returned,* and so informed me. As soon as I became apprised of the fact I sent a telegram to Captain Nance, assistant adjutant-general, notifying him of it (italics added).[16]

While nearly all writers have assumed that the *Hunley* sank with all hands alongside the *Housatonic,* at least one writer has suggested that Lieutenant Dixon actually made it back to Charleston. This rather bold claim was based on an article, "The Torpedo Scare," by Hobart Pacha, which appeared in *Blackwood's Magazine* for June 1885:

I remember on one occasion during the war when I was at Charleston, meeting in a coffee-room at that place a young naval officer (a Southerner), with whom I got into conversation. He told me that that night he was going to sink a Northern man-of-war which was blockading the port, and invited me to see him off. I accompanied him down to his cigar-boat, as he called it, and found that she was a vessel about 40 feet long, shaped like a cigar, on the bow of which was placed a torpedo. On his stepping on board with his crew of four men his boat was immersed till nothing but a small piece of funnel was visible. He moved off into the darkness at no great speed—say at about 5 miles an hour.

The next evening, on visiting the coffee-house, I found my friend sitting quietly smoking his pipe. He told me that he had succeeded in making a hole in the frigate which he had attacked, which vessel could, in fact, be seen lying in shallow water, some 7 miles off, careened over to repair damages. But he said that, on the concussion made by firing the torpedo, the water had rushed in through the hatches of his boat, and she had sunk to the bottom. All his men were drowned. He said he didn't know how he escaped himself, but he fancied that he came up through the hatches, as he found himself floating about, and swam on shore. This affair was officially reported by the American blockading squadron, corroborating the fact of the injury done to the frigate, and stating that the torpedo-boat was got up, with four dead bodies in her hold.

However, it is obvious for the following reasons that Pacha was actually referring to one of the *David* torpedo boats and not the *Hunley.* First, the *Housatonic* was entirely sunk and remained so—it was never "careened over to repair damages." Second, Pacha's reference to a crew of four men would point to a *David*, not the *Hunley*, which had nine men on board. Third, the "funnel" that Pacha saw would imply the smokestack of a *David*, not one of the two hatches characteristic of the *Hunley.* And last, the naval officer with whom Pacha spoke could not have been Lieutenant Dixon, as Dixon was never again seen after the *Housatonic* attack. Had Lieutenant Dixon made it back to shore, surely he would have reported to the Confederate authorities.

So once again the question surfaces: What happened to the *H. L. Hunley?* Apparently the *Hunley* survived the successful attack upon the *Housatonic*, gave the agreed-upon signal, and was actually returning to port when some disaster befell the little craft. What could have happened?

According to eyewitness accounts, the submarine was met with a barrage of small-arms fire as it approached the target. "After I gave the orders to go to quarters several muskets were fired at it, and when it was close alongside Captain Pickering fired his gun at it," reported Officer of the Deck Crosby.

Landsman C. P. Slade testified: "I then started aft; and fired at it out of the starboard port of the pivot gun between the fore and main masts, it being then about 10 yards from the starboard quarter, and moving towards the ship's side."

Executive Officer Higginson also fired at the submarine. "I then went down from the bridge and took the rifle from the lookout on the horseblock on the starboard quarter, and fired it at this object," he testified. "I then took the rifle from the lookout on the port quarter, returned to the starboard quarter, and attempted to fire at the object with this piece from the horseblock, but it missed fire. I then laid it down on the horseblock, stepped down on the deck, and immediately afterwards an explosion took place."

No doubt most of the shots that were fired glanced harmlessly off the *Hunley*'s iron hull. But some of the projectiles may have struck the thick panes of glass set in the hatch combings for observation. Perhaps the little submarine was returning to port, lumbering along the surface of the water, when a capricious wave slapped against the hatch combings. The weakened glass might have given way, sending splinters and foaming water cascading below. The *Hunley* possessed such little freeboard, only a few seconds of such flooding would be required to send it irreversibly to the bottom.

Of course this is pure speculation. If the wreck of the *Hunley* is ever found, perhaps more will be learned. But with each passing day a little more of the *Hunley* turns to rust and is swept away by the ocean currents. Soon there will be nothing left but conjecture.

Repercussions of the submarine attack reverberated throughout the North. Admiral Dahlgren was shocked at the deadly blow the little *Hunley* had dealt the *Housatonic*. On February 19, 1864, he wrote to Gideon Welles, Secretary of the Navy: "The Department will readily perceive the consequences likely to result from this event; the whole line of blockade will be infested with these cheap, convenient, and formidable defenses, and we must guard every point. The measures for prevention may not be so obvious."[17] On the same day, Admiral Dahlgren issued the following order:

> The success of this undertaking will, no doubt, lead to similar attempts along the whole line of blockade.
> If vessels on blockade are at anchor they are not safe, particularly in smooth water, without outriggers and hawsers stretched around with rope netting dropped in the water.
> Vessels on inside blockade had better take post outside at night and keep underway, until these preparations are completed.
> All the boats must be on the patrol when the vessel is not in motion.[18]

The once-confident vessels of the Federal blockading fleet still dominated Charleston harbor by day. But by night, the ships sought refuge outside the harbor, huddling together for mutual protection, hoping to avoid the terrible underwater menace lurking below.

Back in Charleston, the Confederate authorities anxiously awaited news of the *Hunley* and its crew. Perhaps they had been captured. Perhaps they had been swept out to sea. Day passed after day, and still no news. How the *Housatonic* was sunk was not known in Charleston until February 27, when Federal prisoners, captured in a picket boat, divulged the facts.[19] On February 29, 1864, the *Charleston Mercury* printed the following account of the *Hunley*'s attack upon the *Housatonic:*

> The news this morning from our immediate vicinity is quite as cheering as that which is echoed along the wires from the far off battle fields of Georgia and the Southwest.
>
> An official dispatch was received from Colonel Elliott at Fort Sumter, on Saturday, conveying the gratifying news that one of our picket boats, commanded by boatswain Smith, had captured a Yankee picket boat containing one officer and five men. The prisoners have arrived in the city. Their accounts of the success of the pioneer of our fleet of torpedo boats are really exhilarating. They state that the vessel sunk off the harbor on the night of the 16th, and reported lost in a gale, was the U.S. steamer *Housatonic,* carrying 12 guns and three hundred men, and that she was blown up by our torpedo boat.
>
> This fine and powerful vessel was sunk in three minutes. The whole stern of the steamer was blown off by the explosion. All of the crew of the *Housatonic* are said to have been saved, except five—two officers and three men—who are missing and supposed to be drowned. As a practical and important result of this splendid achievement, the prisoners state that all the wooden vessels of the blockading squadron now go far out to sea every night, being afraid of the risk of riding at anchor in any portion of the outer harbor.
>
> The torpedo boat that has accomplished this glorious exploit was under the command of Lieutenant Dixon. We are glad to be able to assure our readers that the boat and crew are now safe.

An even more glowing account of the *Hunley*'s attack appeared in the *Charleston Daily Courier* for the same date:

On Friday night about half past 9 o'clock one of our naval picket boats, under command of Boatswain J. M. Smith, captured a Yankee picket boat off Fort Sumter containing 1 commissioned officer and 5 men. . . . The officer taken prisoner is Midshipman William H. Kitching, acting master's mate of the United States blockading steamer *Nipsic.* The rest of the prisoners are landsmen.

By the prisoners we learn that the blockader sunk by our torpedo boat on the night of the 16th instant was the United States steam sloop-of-war *Housatonic,* carrying 12 guns and a crew of 300 men. They state that the torpedo boat, cigar shape, was first seen approaching by the watch on board the *Housatonic.* The alarm was given, and immediately all hands beat to quarters.

A rapid musketry fire was opened upon the boat, but without effect. Being unable to depress their guns, the order was given to slip the cable. In doing this, the *Housatonic* backed some distance and came in collision with the cigar boat. The torpedo exploded almost immediately, carrying away the whole stern of the vessel. The steamer sunk in three minutes' time, the officers and crew barely escaping to the rigging. Everything else on board—guns, stores, ammunition, etc., together with the small boats—went down with her.

The explosion made no noise and the affair was not known among the fleet until daybreak, when the crew was discovered and released from their uneasy positions. They had remained there all night. Two officers and three men are reported missing and supposed to be drowned.

The loss of the *Housatonic* caused great consternation in the fleet. All the wooden vessels are ordered to keep up steam and go out to sea every night, not being allowed to anchor inside. The picket boats have been doubled and the force in each boat increased.

This glorious success of our little torpedo boat under the command of Lieutenant Dixon, of Mobile, has raised the hopes of our people, and the most sanguine expectations are now entertained of our being able to raise the siege in a way little dreamed of by the enemy.

The siege was never lifted, the blockade never broken. One year after the *Hunley*'s epic-making attack, Charleston's weakened defenses fell. The Confederacy succumbed to the Union's overpowering force shortly thereafter. The war, with all its trials and tribulations, was finally over.

But the *H. L. Hunley* had made its mark upon history, ushering in an entirely new era of naval warfare. On January 27, 1958, Rear Admiral Frederick B. Warder, Commander of the Atlantic Submarine Force, presented historian Eustace Williams's collection of documents pertaining to the *Hunley* to Commander William R. Anderson, skipper of the *Nautilus*, the first atomic-powered submarine. Rear Admiral Warder's remarks at that ceremony do final justice to the *Hunley*:

> We in submarines owe *Hunley* a great deal, but the fact this crude vessel was the forerunner of present underseas warfare isn't the only important aspect of the 19th Century boat. The *Hunley* was the first submarine ever to sink a warship in combat—blasting a gaping hole in the side of the Union frigate *Housatonic* and sending her shockingly to the bottom. . . .
>
> This little boat taught man a great deal by her short and tragic adventure. True, her imperfections were many and her success in combat scant and fatal, but she set a precedent of world shaking consequence. By sinking that Union ship, *Hunley* demonstrated that a ship could veil herself in the underwater world and, through the element of surprise, deal an enemy a deadly blow. *This was the beginning of a drastic change—a brilliant revolution—in sea warfare* (italics added).

No one knows for sure what happened to the battle-worn submarine or its brave crew. The wreck of the *Hunley* has never been located. To this day it lies hidden somewhere beneath the green waters off Charleston harbor. And within the rusting confines of its once-sleek hull remain the bodies of its devoted crew: men who gave their lives for a cause they believed in and a dream pursued.

Notes

CHAPTER 1

1. W. M. Robinson, Jr., *The Confederate Privateers* (New Haven, Conn.: Yale University Press, 1928).

2. Ibid., p. 167.

3. J. T. Scharf, *History of the Confederate States Navy* (Albany, N.Y.: Joseph McDonough, 1894), p. 750.

4. James McClintock's undated letter to Matthew F. Maury. Found in Vol. 46 of the Matthew F. Maury Papers, items 9087-9094, Manuscript Division, Library of Congress.

5. *Official Records of the Union and Confederate Navies in the War of the Rebellion* (Washington, D.C., 1901), Series 1, 9, pp. 399–400.

6. R. Duncan, *The Captain and Submarine CSS H. L. Hunley* (Memphis, Tenn.: S. C. Toof, 1965), p. 39.

7. Ibid., p. 19.

8. W. A. Alexander, "The True Stories of the Confederate Submarine Boats," *New Orleans Picayune*, June 29, 1902.

9. Louis Genella Collection, Special Collections Division, Tulane University.

10. Ibid.

11. Robinson, *Confederate Privateers*, pp. 172–74.

12. G. W. Baird, "Submarine Torpedo Boats," *Journal of American Societies of Naval Engineers*, 14, 3 (1902), pp. 845–46.

13. S. Lake, *The Submarine in War and Peace* (Philadelphia: J. B. Lippincott, 1918), pp. 39–40.

14. Ibid., pp. 152–53.

CHAPTER 2

1. W. A. Alexander, "The True Stories of the Confederate Submarine Boats," *New Orleans Picayune*, June 29, 1902.

2. James McClintock's undated letter to Matthew F. Maury. Found in Vol. 46 of the Matthew Maury Papers, items 9087–9094, Manuscript Division, Library of Congress.

3. Ibid.

4. Alexander, "Submarine Boats."

5. *The War of the Rebellion: A Compilation of the Official Records of the Union and Confederate Armies* (Washington, D.C., 1901), 26, Series 1, Pt. 2, pp. 173–74, hereinafter cited as *Army Records*.

6. R. Duncan, *The Captain and Submarine CSS H. L. Hunley* (Memphis, Tenn.: S. C. Toof, 1965), p. 64.

7. McClintock to Maury, Maury Papers.

8. Alexander, "Submarine Boats."

9. *Army Records*, Series 1, 28, Pt. 2, p. 265.

10. *Official Records of the Union and Confederate Navies in the War of the Rebellion* (Washington, D.C., 1901), Series 1, 15, p. 229, hereinafter cited as *Navy Records*.

11. *Army Records*, Series 1, 28, Pt. 2, p. 285.

12. Duncan, *Captain and Submarine Hunley*, pp. 65–66.

13. C. H. Olmstead, "Reminiscences of Service in Charleston Harbor in 1863," *Southern Historical Society Papers*, 11 (1883), pp. 120–21.

14. Ibid.

15. Ibid.

16. *Army Records*, Series 1, 28, Pt. 2, p. 670.

17. Ibid.

18. Ibid., p. 376.

19. Ibid., Pt. 1, p. 551.

20. C. L. Stanton, "Submarines and Torpedo Boats," *Confederate Veteran*, 22 (1914), p. 398.

21. W. B. Fort, "First Submarine in the Confederate Navy," *Confederate Veteran*, 26 (1918), p. 459.

22. National Archives, Confederate Records.

23. National Archives, Record Group 109, Letters Received #222.

24. Ibid., Letters Received #223.

25. Alexander, "Submarine Boats."

26. Ibid.

27. G. T. Beauregard, "Torpedo Service in the Harbor and Water Defenses of Charleston," *Southern Historical Society Papers*, 5, 4 (1878), p. 153.

28. Ibid.

29. *Navy Records*, Series 1, 15, p. 692.

30. Beauregard, "Torpedo Service," p. 153.

31. Alexander, "Submarine Boats."

32. *Navy Records*, Series 1, 15, pp. 334–35.

33. Beauregard, "Torpedo Service," pp. 153–54.

34. *Navy Records*, Series 1, 15, p. 229.

35. *Army Records*, Series 1, 28, p. 553.

36. Alexander, "Submarine Boats."

37. McClintock to Maury, Maury Papers.

38. *Navy Records*, Series 1, 26, pp. 187–89.

39. Alexander, "Submarine Boats."

40. S. Lake, *The Submarine in War and Peace* (Philadelphia: J. B. Lippincott, 1918).

41. Used with permission of Mr. Caldwell Delaney, Director of City of Mobile Museum Department.

42. Alexander, "Submarine Boats."

CHAPTER 3

1. *Official Records of the Union and Confederate Navies in the War of the Rebellion* (Washington, D.C., 1901), Series 1, 6, p. 363, hereinafter cited as *Navy Records*.

2. Ibid., pp. 392–93.

3. Ibid., Series 1, 19, p. 628.

4. Louis Genella Collection, Special Collections Division, Tulane University.

5. *Navy Records*, Series 1, 9, pp. 411–12.

6. National Archives, Squadron Letters, microcopy 89, roll 147, p. 370.

7. Ibid., p. 370a.

8. Ibid., p. 369.

9. *Navy Records*, Series 1, 15, p. 332.

CHAPTER 4

1. W. A. Alexander, "The True Stories of the Confederate Submarine Boats," *New Orleans Picayune*, June 29, 1902.

2. *Official Records of the Union and Confederate Navies in the War of the Rebellion* (Washington, D.C., 1901), Series 1, 15, p. 334, hereinafter cited as *Navy Records*.

3. National Archives, *Proceedings of the Naval Court of Inquiry*, Case #4345.

4. *Navy Records*, Series 1, 15, p. 328.

5. G. T. Beauregard, "Torpedo Service in the Harbor and Water Defenses of Charleston," *Southern Historical Society Papers*, 5, 4 (1878), p. 153.

6. Alexander, "Submarine Boats."

7. M. F. Perry, *Infernal Machines* (Baton Rouge, La.: Louisiana State University Press, 1965).

8. *Navy Records*, Series 1, 26, p. 188.

9. *The War of the Rebellion: A Compilation of the Official Records of the Union and Confederate Armies* (Washington, D.C., 1901), Series 1, 26, Pt. 2, pp. 173–74 hereinafter cited as *Army Records*.

10. National Archives, Squadron Letters, microcopy 89, roll 147, p. 58.

11. *Army Records*, Series 1, 26, Pt. 2, p. 180.

12. *Navy Records*, Series 1, 15, p. 331.

13. Ibid., p. 334.

14. *Annual Report of Major Q. A. Gillmore, Corps of Engineers, for the Fiscal Year Ending June 30, 1872*, Appendix S, pp. 6–7.

15. J. N. Cordozo, *Reminiscences Charleston* (Charleston, S.C.: Joseph Walker, 1866), pp. 124–25.

16. *Navy Records*, Series 1, 15, p. 335.

17. Ibid., p. 329.

18. Ibid., p. 330.

19. Ibid., p. 332.

Bibliography

"Admiral Dietrich Hauls Down His Flag of Command Here." *Charleston News and Courier*, June 16, 1957.

Alexander, W. A. "The Confederate Submarine Torpedo Boat *Hunley.*" *Gulf States Historical Magazine*, September 1902, pp. 81–91.

Alexander, W. A. "The Heroes of the *Hunley.*" *Munsey Magazine*, August 1903, pp. 746–49.

Alexander, W. A. "Thrilling Chapter in the History of the Confederate States Navy." *Southern Historical Society Papers*, 1902, 30, 164–74.

Alexander, W. A. "The True Stories of the Confederate Submarine Boats." *New Orleans Picayune*, June 29, 1902.

Ammen, D. *The Atlantic Coast.* New York: Charles Scribner's Sons, 1883.

Anderson, B. *By Sea and by River.* New York: Alfred A. Knopf, 1962.

Annual Report of Major Q. A. Gillmore, Corps of Engineers, for the Fiscal Year Ending June 30, 1872. Washington, D.C.: U.S. Government.

Arthur, S. C. "Early New Orleans Submarine Sired *Davids.*" *New Orleans Times Picayune*, Sunday, June 14, 1942.

Arthur, S. C. *New Orleans Item*, December 4, 1921.

Baird, G. W. "Submarine Torpedo Boats." *Journal of American Societies of Naval Engineers*, 1902, 15, 845–55.

Barnes, J. S. *Submarine Warfare, Offensive and Defensive.* New York: D. Van Nostrand Co., 1869.

Baumgartner, B. "The First Submarine." *Gulf Soundings*, January 1967, pp. 4, 6.

Beard, W. E. "The Confederate Submarine." In W. Adolphe Roberts and Lowell Brentano (eds.), *The Book of the Navy.* New York: Doubleday, 1944.

Beard, W. E. "The Log of the C.S. Submarine." *U.S. Naval Institute Proceedings,* 1916, 42, 1545–57.

Beauregard, G. T. "Torpedo Service in Charleston Harbor. *Annals of the War Written by Leading Participants North and South.* Philadelphia: Times Publishing Co., 1879.

Beauregard, G. T. "Torpedo Service in the Harbor and Water Defences of Charleston." *Southern Historical Society Papers,* April 1878, pp. 145–61.

Beauregard, G. T. "Water Defences of Charleston." *Philadelphia Weekly Times,* October 6, 1877, p. 1.

Blair, C. H. "Submarines of the Confederate Navy." *U.S. Naval Institute Proceedings,* October 1952, pp. 1115–21.

Bowman, B. "The *Hunley*: Ill-fated Confederate Submarine." *Civil War History,* September 1959, pp. 315–19.

Burgoyne, A. H. *Submarine Navigation: Past and Present.* New York: E. P. Dutton, 1903.

Burton, E. M. *The Siege of Charleston.* Columbia, S.C.: University of South Carolina Press, 1970.

Cardozo, J. N. *Reminiscences Charleston.* Charleston, S.C.: Joseph Walker, 1866.

Charleston Daily Courier, October 16, 1863.

Charleston Mercury, February 29, 1864.

Charleston News and Courier, May 10, 1899.

Civil War Naval Chronology, 1861–1865. Washington, D.C.: U.S. Government Printing Office, 1971.

"Confederates Built First Successful Submarine Boat." *Montgomery Alabama Advertiser,* May 26, 1907.

Crowley, R. O. "The Confederate Torpedo Service." *Century,* June 1898, p. 299.

Davis, B. *The Civil War: Strange and Fascinating Facts.* New York: Fairfax Press, 1982. (Originally published: *Our Incredible Civil War.* New York: Holt, Rinehart & Winston, 1960.)

Ditmars, C. *"Hunley* Wrote History Though Cause Was Lost." *Mobile Press Register,* Sunday, May 5, 1957.

Doran, C. "First Submarine in Actual Warfare." *Confederate Veteran,* 1908, 16, 71–72.

Dorset, P. F. "CSS *Pioneer."* In *Historic Ships Afloat.* New York: Macmillan Co., 1967, pp. 126–30.

Duncan, R. H. *The Captain and Submarine CSS H.L. Hunley.* Memphis, Tenn.: S. C. Toof and Co., 1965.

Durkin, J. T. *Stephen R. Mallory: Confederate Navy Chief.* Chapel Hill, N.C.: University of North Carolina Press, 1954.

Field, C. *The Story of the Submarine: From the Earliest Ages to the Present Day.* London: Sampson Low, Marston and Co., 1908.

"Fire on Submarine Here Extinguished." *New Orleans Times Picayune*, March 27, 1966.

"First Torpedo Boat." *New Orleans Picayune*, April 2, 1909.

Ford, A. P. "The First Submarine Boat." *Confederate Veteran*, 1908, 16, 563–64.

Ford, A. P. *Life in the Confederate Army.* New York: Neale Publishing Co., 1905.

Fort, W. B. "First Submarine in the Confederate Navy." *Confederate Veteran*, 1918, 26, 459–60.

Foster, J. "Is the Submarine in the Arcade of the Presbytere Really the *Pioneer?*" *New Orleans Times Picayune*, May 14, 1961 (Dixie Roto Section).

Fyfe, H. C. *Submarine Warfare: Past and Present.* New York: E. P. Dutton, 1907.

Louis Genella Collection. Tulane University.

Hagerman, G. "Confederate Submarines." *U.S. Naval Institute Proceedings*, September 1977, pp. 74–75.

Harper's Weekly, November 2, 1861, p. 701.

Hill, H. N. "Texan Gave World First Successful Submarine Torpedo." *San Antonio Express*, July 30, 1916.

Hoyt, E. P. *From the Turtle to the Nautilus: The Story of Submarines.* Boston: Little, Brown & Co., 1963.

"*Hunley-Pioneer* Puzzles." *New Orleans Times Picayune*, December 4, 1967.

The Hunley. Pamphlet by South Carolina Confederate War Centennial Commission. Aiken, S.C.

Johnson, J. *The Defense of Charleston Harbor.* Charleston, S.C.: Walker, Evans and Cogswell, 1890.

Kelln, A. L. "Confederate Submarines." *Virginia Magazine of History and Biography*, July 1953, pp. 293–303.

Kitchen, R. P., Jr. "Saga of the C.S.S. *Hunley.*" *Sea Classics*, July 1984.

von Kolnitz, H. "The Confederate Submarine." *U.S. Naval Institute Proceedings*, October 1937, pp. 1453–57; 1466–68.

Lake, S. *The Submarine in War and Peace: Its Development and Its Possibilities.* Philadelphia: J. B. Lippincott Co., 1918.

Letters Received by the Secretary of the Navy from Commanding Officers of Squadrons (Scquephen R. Mallory: Confederate Navy Chief. Chapel Hill, N.C.: University of North Carolina Press, 1954.

Levy, G. S. "Torpedo Boat at Louisiana Solders' Home." *Confederate Veteran,* 1909, 17, 459.

Little, R. H. "The First Submarine to Sink a Hostile Warship." *Chicago Tribune,* November 29, 1936.

McClintock, J. Undated letter to Matthew F. Maury. Maury Papers, Library of Congress, Washington, D.C.

Mazet, H. S. "Tragedy and the Confederate Submarines." *U.S. Naval Institute Proceedings,* May 1942, pp. 663-68.

Mustard, E. C. "The Submarine in the Revolution and Civil War," *Social Studies,* May 1946, pp. 204-10.

Nash, H. P., Jr. *Naval History of the Civil War.* New York: A. S. Barnes and Co., 1972.

"Nautilus Gets Papers on Confederate *Hunley.*" *Charleston News and Courier,* January 28, 1958.

"Nautilus to Get *Hunley* History." *Charleston News and Courier,* January 25, 1958.

"Navy Still Plans Hunt for *Hunley.*" *Charleston News and Courier,* August 28, 1957.

New Orleans Times Picayune, February 15, 1868.

Olmstead, C. H. "Reminiscences of Service in Charleston Harbor in 1863." *Southern Historical Society Papers,* 1883, 11, 118-25; 158-71.

"Our Torpedo Boat." *Southern Historical Society Papers,* 1901, 29, 292-95.

Pacha, H. "The Torpedo Scare." *Blackwood's Magazine,* June 1885, pp. 745-46.

Perry, M. F. *Infernal Machines.* Louisiana State University Press, 1965.

Porter, D. D. *Naval History of the Civil War.* New York: Sherman, 1886.

Proceedings of the Naval Court of Inquiry. Case #4345, February 26, 1864, National Archives, Washington, D.C.

Rebellion Record 1860-61. Document #175, "Submarine Boat at Philadelphia."

Roberts, W. A. *Lake Pontchartrain.* Indianapolis: Bobbs-Merrill Co., 1946, pp. 257-59.

Robinson, W. M., Jr. *The Confederate Privateers.* New Haven: Yale University Press, 1928.

Roman, A. *General Beauregard,* New York: Harper, 1884.

"Salvage of Submarine *Hunley* Has Chance for Success." *Charleston News and Courier,* June 18, 1957.

Scharf, J. T. *History of the Confederate States Navy.* Albany, N.Y.: Joseph McDonough, 1894.

Scheliha, V. von. *A Treatise on Coast Defense.* London, 1868 (reprinted in 1971 by Greenwood Press, Westport, Conn.).

Shugg, W. "Prophet of the Deep: The *H.L. Hunley.*" *Civil War Times,* 1973, 11, 4–10; 44–47.

Sims, L. "The Submarine That Wouldn't Come Up." *American Heritage,* 1958, 8, 48–51; 107–11.

Smythe Letters. South Carolina Historical Society, Charleston, S.C.

Stanton, C. L. "Submarines and Torpedo Boats." *Confederate Veteran,* 1914, 22, 398–99.

Stern, P. *The Confederate Navy.* New York: Bonanza Books, 1962.

Sueter, M. F. *The Evolution of the Submarine Boat.* Portsmouth, England: J. Griffin and Co., 1907.

Thomson, D. W. "Three Confederate Submarines." *U.S. Naval Institute Proceedings,* January 1941, pp. 39–47.

Tomb, J. H. "Submarines and Torpedo Boats, C.S.N." *Confederate Veteran,* 1914, 22, 168–69.

Villard, O. S. "The Submarine and the Torpedo in the Blockade of the Confederacy." *Harper's Monthly,* June 1916, pp. 131–37.

Walker, R. "Peripatetic Coffin." *South Atlantic Quarterly,* October 1940, pp. 438–47.

The War of the Rebellion: A Compilation of the Official Records of the Union and Confederate Armies. Washington, D.C.: U.S. Government Printing Office, 1901.

Wilkinson, D. "Peripatetic Coffin." *Oceans,* #4, 1978.

Eustace Williams Collection. Emory University, Atlanta, Georgia.

Willis, E. *Torpedoes and Torpedo Boats* (unpublished manuscript). Manuscript Division, Library of Congress, Washington, D.C.

Index

About the Author

James E. Kloeppel was born in Sioux City, Iowa, on November 19, 1954. The clean air and dark Iowa nights nurtured his early interest in astronomy. After receiving a physics degree from Morningside College, Mr. Kloeppel moved to Tucson, Arizona, where he worked as a technician at Kitt Peak National Observatory. Much of the historical information for his first book, *Realm of the Long Eyes*, was gathered while he lived at the mountain-based observatory.

Mr. Kloeppel's technical background also includes work as a technician at the Sommers-Bausch Observatory of the University of Colorado, as a technician at the Georgia Tech Research Institute, and as an engineering writer for General Dynamics. He is currently employed as a science writer at the Georgia Institute of Technology.